# BRITISH RAILWAYS

## PAST and PRESENT

## No 16

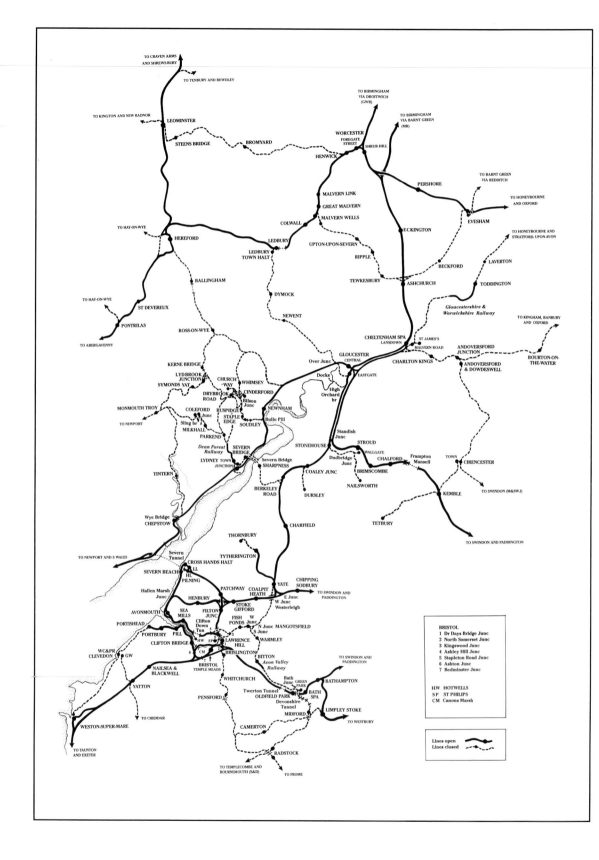

# BRITISH RAILWAYS

# PAST and PRESENT

# No 16

## Avon, Cotswolds and the Malverns
### Hereford & Worcester, Gloucestershire and Avon

## Geoff Dowling and John Whitehouse

Past and
Present

Past & Present Publishing Ltd

First published in 1993
Reprinted 1993
Reprinted 1995
Reprinted 2001

British Library Cataloguing in Publication Data

A catalogue record for this book is available from the
British Library

ISBN 1 85895 077 5

Past & Present Publishing Ltd
The Trundle
Ringstead Road
Great Addington
Kettering
Northants
NN14 4BW

Tel/Fax: 01536 330588
email: sales@nostalgiacollection.com
Website: www.nostalgiacollection.com

The research and captions are by John Whitehouse;
photographic printing by Geoff Dowling

Maps drawn by Christina Siviter

Printed and bound in Great Britain

**BATH GREEN PARK:** The view from
the top of the steps of Bath Station
signal box looking towards the station. BR 'Standard' 2-6-4T No 80138
has just crossed the River Avon
bridge with the 1.10 pm local to
Templecombe and is passing the
original Midland Railway Shed on
the left. Note the old coach body
(far left) which was used by the
men of Bath Depot for their Mutual
Improvement Classes. In the station
stands 'Peak' Class diesel-electric
No D88 on a local train to Bristol.
This view was taken on 20 October
1965, and the redevelopment of
central Bath was well in hand, with
a slab-sided government office
block already obstructing the view
of Bath Abbey.

Following closure in 1966, Green
Park's future was uncertain,
despite having Grade 2 listed building status. Eventually supermarket
giant J. Sainsbury stepped in to pre-
serve the building as part of their
new superstore complex. The
extent of Sainsbury's operation is
clearly evident from this view, with
car parking and their garden centre
occupying the site of the engine
shed and goods yard. This photograph was taken from the roof of a
partially completed office block
and ironically is very close to the
position of the original photographer in both location and elevation. In
the background can be seen further
city centre development, whilst the
main retail store is on the right.
(See also page 95) *Hugh
Ballantyne/GD*

# CONTENTS

# BIBLIOGRAPHY

Rail Atlas of Great Britain & Ireland *by S. K. Baker (OPC)*
A Pictorial Record of Great Western Architecture *by A. Vaughan (OPC)*
The Railway Heritage of Britain *by Gordon Biddle & O. S. Nock (Michael Joseph)*
The Banbury & Cheltenham Railway 1887-1962 *by J. H. Russell (OPC)*
A Pictorial Record of Great Western Engines *by J. H. Russell (OPC)*
Nameplates of the Big Four *by Frank Burridge (OPC)*
Bradshaws Railway Guide (reprint) *(David & Charles)*
Passengers No More *by Gerald Daniels & L. A. Dench (Ian Allan)*
Branch lines of Gloucester *by Colin Maggs (Alan Sutton)*

Diesel Hydraulic Locomotives of the Western Region *by Brian Reed (David & Charles)*
A Regional History of the Railways of Great Britain, Vol 1 The West Country *by David St John Thomas & Allan Patmore (David & Charles)*
    Vol 7 The West Midlands *by Rex Christiansen*
    Vol 13 Thames & Severn *by Rex Christiansen*
Rail Centres: Bristol *by Colin Maggs (Ian Allan)*
Railways of the Cotswolds *by Colin Maggs* (Peter Nicholson)
The Western Region before Beeching *by Chris Leigh (Ian Allan)*
The Severn & Wye Railway, Vols 1-3 *by Ian Pope, Bob How and Paul Karau (Wild Swan)*

LYDNEY TOWN: A little of the Steam Age lives on in the Forest of Dean. Push-pull fitted ex-GWR 0-4-2T No 1431 stands in the up platform at Lydney Town on 4 June 1960 with an auto-train for Berkeley Road (via the Severn Railway Bridge). The building on the right is of Great Western origin dating back to 1897, whilst those on the up platform are of original Severn & Wye construction. Note, too, the station nameboard of Midland Railway origin, firmly establishing the joint ownership of the line. Lydney also enjoyed the use of two other stations: the Junction Station, again of Severn & Wye origin, and the GW station on the South Wales main line, the two being linked by a spur. The Severn & Wye branch to Lydney Docks crossed the main line at right angles on the flat at the south end of the GW station. Of the three, Town was the most convenient for the local population.

The station area has been redeveloped, but trains (courtesy of the Dean Forest Railway Preservation Society) still pass. Note the original platform face which survives today, being the only connection with the past. The train is headed by a Hunslet 0-6-0ST 'Austerity' returning from Lydney Lakeside to Norchard. The preservation society plans to re-open the station in the near future. *Hugh Ballantyne/GD*

# INTRODUCTION

Flushed with success on the completion of our last 'Past and Present' book, we readily agreed to do another. After all, we said, it must be easier the second time - we knew all the pitfalls, all the problems, it would be a breeze!

Wrong! Our chosen area seems to have had more published about it in the past than any other; Bristol books abound, volumes have been written on the Birmingham to Gloucester Railway, and the Forest of Dean has been covered in minute detail. All very well, but it depletes the stock of unused archive material. Not all was gloom though. Along the way we were lucky and made contact with some splendid photographers who trusted us with their material, in most cases irreplaceable original negatives. We hope the end results justify their faith!

As ever when producing a 'Past and Present book', if the line was long closed a running battle took place between photographer and vegetation (or in the case of Gloucester the motor vehicle). Imagine, then, the joy of finding, on the long-mothballed Portishead branch, that the footbridge overlooking Clifton Bridge station was still there, and how short-lived that joy was when we discovered that all the steps had been taken out! At Mangotsfield we had an encounter with 'New Age Travellers' who had set up camp on the old trackbed along which we had to walk to reach the junction. After establishing that we were not council officials, they treated us to a fine display of Indian club juggling.

The area we cover in this volume is one of great contrasts; to the west is the peace and tranquillity of the Forest of Dean National Park with its two small towns of Cinderford and Coleford set deep in the forest, but only a short journey across the Severn Bridge soon brings the traveller into the sprawling city of Bristol with its station, Temple Meads, the hub of our area, from where we visit the seaside towns of Weston-super-Mare and Clevedon.

A brief run of 21 minutes by HST from Bristol takes us on to the magnificent Georgian city of Bath where Brunel had to twice cross the River Avon with his railway and the Somerset & Dorset still lives on in the sensitively restored Green Park station. Elsewhere in the area we briefly visit Hereford, where the GWR and LNWR jointly owned the station, and Cheltenham, to explore the branch as far as Bourton-on-the-Water, so choked with road traffic these days. From Cheltenham it was also possible to travel, by main line, towards Stratford. Genteel Cheltenham, so different to its more cosmopolitan neighbour Gloucester. It was at Gloucester that the Broad Gauge of the GWR met with the standard gauge of the Midland, with chaotic results for the traveller who had to change trains with all his baggage.

At the top of the area is Worcester, cathedral city and gateway to the scenic beauty of the Malverns. From there it is a gentle amble along long-lifted branch lines, back into the Forest of Dean.

The railways in the area have suffered savage cuts over the years. The Forest of Dean had a large network of lines serving a maze of quarries and mines together with a good passenger network; now, apart from the Gloucester to South Wales line skirting its southern edge, it has nothing, although the Dean Forest Railway does recreate some of the lost scene. Many small towns have lost their railway line or station, often just before they expanded with the shift of population away from larger towns and cities; among these are Tewkesbury, Bromyard, Chipping Sodbury, Monmouth and Radstock. Where the line still exists it is, however, possible to reverse the process. This has happened at Yate, where a new station has attracted much new business; unfortunately, also at Yate the line to Tytherington quarry has had to be mothballed because of the current economic situation.

Main lines that have been lost include the Midland line to Bath and the GW line from Birmingham to Cheltenham via Stratford, although part of both of these lines have attracted preservation societies with, respectively, the Gloucester & Warwickshire Railway Society at Toddington and the Bitton Railway near Bristol.

The aim of this book is not to produce a comprehensive historical or pictorial record of this area - that has been done well before. Its aim is to provide the reader with an interesting series of comparisons of familiar and not so familiar views. We hope that it may encourage an interest in railways away from the usual railway enthusiast body. Indeed, the old trackbeds in the Forest of Dean and the cycleways between Bristol and Bath provide ample opportunity to inspect some of the scenes in this book at leisure. We also hope that it may stir some pleasant memories of a more gentle age, when it was possible to visit towns, villages and beauty spots without the need for a car.

We would like to thank all those photographers who provided us with the 'past' photographs, the true inspiration for the book, who have been credited in the text, and also the land and property owners who have allowed access to their properties when taking the 'present' pictures.

**Geoff Dowling ARPS**
**John Whitehouse**

**Acknowledgements**
Thanks are due to the individuals and organisations that have helped with research, including Chepstow Museum, The Brunel Engineering Trust, Colin Maggs and Richard Strange. As with all such projects, the need to convert the writers' virtually indecipherable scrawl into meaningful text is paramount, and the patience and tenacity of Lorraine Keyte, Pat Neville and Daphne Whitehouse for typing and Jean Dowling for proof-reading is acknowledged with grateful thanks.

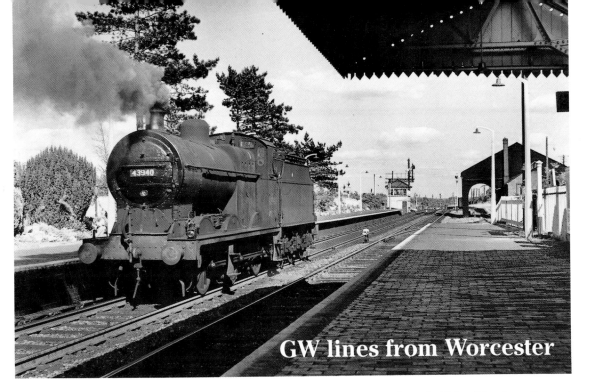

# GW lines from Worcester

PERSHORE: There were four intermediate stations to the east of Worcester along the Vale of Evesham, the most important of which was Pershore. In fact, the station was located some 1 mile to the north of this busy market town, and enjoyed extensive goods facilities reflecting the important market gardening activities in the area. In this June 1961 scene, goods facilities are evident on both sides of the main line as Class '4F' 0-6-0 No 43940 passes running tender-first towards Evesham. At this time the 'Cotswolds line', as it was known, was part of an important cross-country route which linked the east, via Bedford, Bletchley and Oxford, to the conurbations in the west served by the Birmingham to Bristol main line.

Pershore alone survived when the remaining intermediate stations closed in 1966, albeit in a much rationalised state. The station buildings and goods shed were swept away and the track singled, reflecting the loss of the important freight traffic. Today only the fencing, lighting and remains of the up platform recall its more prosperous past. A stopping service comprised of Class '150/2' 'Sprinter' No 150266 approaches.
*Ellis James-Robertson/GD*

WORCESTER SHRUB HILL: Worcester was originally by-passed by the Birmingham-Bristol main line, and joined the railway map when the Oxford, Worcester & Wolverhampton (usually known as the 'Old Worse and Worse') laid a connection from the city to the main line in 1850. Two years later the Worcester Loop was completed with a connection for the main line at Stoke Works via Droitwich. Shrub Hill Station for many years had an all-over roof as this undated scene records; it was probably taken at around the turn of the century and well illustrates this impressive station. Despite extensive enquiries, the exact date the roof was removed is also unknown, although it is believed to have lasted into the mid-1930s.

The station today presents a neat and tidy appearance, as Class '158' No 158780 departs with a Cardiff to Nottingham train on 31 August 1991. On the left are two Class '37' locomotives from the Civil Engineer's pool with ballast trains for the next day's engineering work. *Collection of Ellis James-Robertson/JW*

MALVERN LINK: One mile north of Great Malvern is Malvern Link, which is mainly a residential community although nearby common land is a popular recreational amenity. The station, which is situated centrally to both, opened in 1859, being the southern end of 6 miles of railway from Henwick, near Worcester. It had one particular advantage over Great Malvern, which was space, so it was possible to develop goods facilities which are well illustrated in this August 1958 view. '94XX' Class 0-6-0PT No 8427 stands in the goods bay whilst a nine-car formation of Swindon 'Cross Country' DMU triple sets heads north with a Cardiff to Birmingham Snow Hill train. Sidings on both sides of the main line indicate ample traffic.

The station remains in use, but the goods facilities have disappeared, the railway now being hemmed in on one side by an industrial estate and on the other by a caravan park. On a June day in 1989, Class '150/1' 'Sprinter' No 150145 approaches with a stopping service for Hereford. *Peter Shoesmith/JW*

COLWALL: The Malvern Hills presented a formidable barrier to the promoters of the Worcester & Hereford Railway. Indeed, a project by the London & North Western Railway to connect the two cathedral cities with a line skirting the Malverns to the north was defeated only by objectors from Great Malvern and Ledbury, the major intervening towns which would not have been served by the projected line. Tunneling itself caused further delays to the opening, and indeed the original single-bore tunnel was later replaced by a somewhat longer tunnel but of a slightly easier gradient. The enormity of the barrier provided by the Malvern Hills can be well judged from this May 1959 photograph, with Class '68XX' 'Grange' No 6853 *Morehampton Grange* heading an express to Hereford. The train has just passed through Colwall station, which was located at the west end of the tunnel.

Class '156' 'Sprinter' No 156415 typifies the new generation of trains on the line, forming a Hereford stopping service. The scene itself is little changed, with the precariously situated half-timbered cottage in the foreground remaining in excellent condition, whilst the background is dominated by the bulk of the Malverns. The route has been partially singled, from Malvern Link to the junction with the 'North and West' route near Hereford. *Peter Shoesmith/JW*

NEAR LEDBURY: The second major tunnel on the route was at Ledbury. Built as a single bore it is approached from the east by a downward gradient. To combat the potential problem of a runaway train, an escape line was constructed which ran along an embankment at the side of the main line. The runaway line is seen here nearest the camera as Class '35' 'Hymek' No D7083 climbs from the tunnel on 16 May 1964 with the 10.05 am Hereford to Paddington train.

Rationalisation brought singling, thus dispensing with the need for the runaway line and the signal box. In May 1989 Class '47' No 47620 *Windsor Castle* sweeps round the curve heading a Sundays-only Paddington-Hereford express. The locomotive's external appearance reflects its use as a favoured Royal Train engine at the time. *Michael Mensing/JW*

LEDBURY engine shed, located alongside the up platform, was a sub-depot to Hereford (85C) and catered mainly for banking engines to assist freights and the occasional passenger train through the narrow-bore single-track tunnel. The tunnel, 1,323 yards in length, had an adverse gradient of 1 in 80 for Worcester-bound trains. On 11 July 1959 Class '42XX' 2-8-0T No 5243 stands by the coaling stage between duties. Note the small turntable which was installed when the branch to Gloucester opened in 1885, used mainly for turning branch-line locomotives. The banking engine usually operated bunker first in order to provide the crew with some meagre relief from the blast of their own engine in the poorly ventilated tunnel.

The coming of dieselisation brought rationalisation, which eliminated the need for banking locomotives, and the shed closed in July 1964. The area has now become overgrown, although the trackbed can be identified. On the extreme right can be seen the main line leading to Ledbury Tunnel mouth. Ledbury is now one of the few remaining pockets of lower quadrant semaphore signalling on the old Western Region. *W. Potter/JW*

LEDBURY TOWN: Until 1959 Ledbury was a junction, with the branch from Gloucester via Newent and Dymock joining the Hereford to Worcester line to the west of the main-line station. Ledbury Town Halt was sited more conveniently for the town, located within easy walking distance of the main street. However, traffic on the single-line branch was not heavy, with a service of five trains each way per day prior to the Grouping. It was perhaps of little surprise that it became an early closure in mid-1959, ahead of the more swingeing Beeching cuts. On 5 August 1958 a '57XX' series 0-6-0PT stands at the Halt with a train from Gloucester.

All trace of the railway has now gone with partial filling in of the trackbed; even the road bridge at the southern end of the station has been removed. At present a public park and recreational ground occupy the site. The left-hand wall and the right-hand factory and iron fence clearly identify the location.
*Peter Shoesmith/JW*

DYMOCK: The charming village of Dymock was some 5¹/₄ miles from Ledbury Town on the line to Gloucester, and its station was situated on a passing loop controlled by one of only three signal boxes on the line. The station building was of typical GW design. In latter years the passenger service was handled mainly by the distinctive ex-GWR railcars, one such being W19W which is seen here pausing at Dymock with the 5.25 pm Ledbury to Gloucester train on 11 July 1959, the last day of the passenger service on the line. The railway from Ledbury to Dymock then closed completely. The lady passenger and the railcar driver are no doubt expressing regret at the loss of the train service.

A retirement home stands on the site of the station building today, and coincidentally the gentleman who can be seen enjoying the afternoon sun happens to be an ex-signalman who manned Dymock signal box just prior to the Second World War. The road overbridge remains, but the course of the railway has been filled in, although the down platform (on the left) survives today as a pathway through the garden area. *Hugh Ballantyne/JW*

NEWENT was the most substantial town on the Ledbury to Gloucester line, although its station is similar in size to that at Dymock, a much smaller settlement. This view again features railcar No W19W working the 5.25 from Ledbury on the last day of service. The line itself had been in decline for many years; it had once been a through route for GW freight between Birmingham and Gloucester until the opening of the shorter Honeybourne line. Following withdrawal of the passenger service the southern section from Dymock remained open until May 1964 for freight services.

When compared with the neat station scene of 1959, it is difficult to believe that this is the same location today. The trackbed is heavily overgrown, as are the two platforms which are now barely evident. It is quite amazing that nature has repossessed this area so quickly. *W. Potter/GD*

BROMYARD: The railway between Worcester and Leominster (featured on page 22) took many years to complete; the original company was formed in 1861 but the line was not completed until 1897. Roughly mid-distance stood Bromyard, reached from Worcester in 1877. Initial plans to complete the line from Leominster had been abandoned some years earlier, but were later reinstated and the Leominster to Steens Bridge stretch opened in 1884, and to Bromyard, to complete the through route, in 1897. Bromyard itself is a busy market town, but the railway struggled. Closure of the western end of the line between Bromyard and Leominster came in 1952, but the remaining section to Worcester survived until 1964. Nine years earlier, on 8 July 1955, ex-GW railcar No W5W prepares to work the 1.58 pm to Worcester. The railcar was of the early series, introduced in 1935 and distinguished from later units by a more rounded front end and no drawbar gear.

The station area has now been engulfed in an industrial estate, with the road bridge (behind the photographer) the only lasting evidence of the railway. The trackbed is now a roadway. *Hugh Ballantyne/JW*

# Hereford and the Welsh Marches

HEREFORD (1): Hereford is a major centre on what is known as the 'North and West' route, which runs from Newport to Shrewsbury and has seen variable fortunes since completion as a through route in 1854. Hereford's importance grew with the completion of rail connections to Ross and Gloucester, Hay on Wye and Worcester. A key operating development was the completion of a spur in 1866 south of Hereford from the Newport to the Ross and Gloucester line giving trains from Newport direct access to Hereford's Barrs Court station, so that north-south trains no longer had to reverse direction. This view is from the end of the northbound platform on 18 May 1957 as 'City' Class 4-4-0 No 3440 *City of Truro* heads '43XX' Class 2-6-0 No 4358 into Hereford with a 'Daffodil Special' railtour. *City of Truro*', accredited with the first recorded attainment of 100 mph in Britain, was withdrawn in 1931 and placed in York Railway Museum. Restored to active use in 1957, in 1961 it was again placed in Swindon Museum, only to re-appear once more in 1985 as part of the GW150 celebrations. Note the British Railways totem on the goods office sign and the footbridge connecting it to the goods shed opposite.

The goods shed remains today, but the goods office has given way to a new trading estate. The avoiding line closed in 1967, but a spur remained to serve a power station and H. P. Bulmers Cider Factory. Bulmers played a key role in the campaign for the return of main-line steam in the early 1970s and a steam centre is located within their complex which is also used to service visiting engines on main-line duty. On 12 October 1992 a more familiar sight approaches Hereford (the Barrs Court name was dropped some time ago) in the shape of Class '37s' No 37274 and 37250 working steel empties from Dee Marsh (near Chester) to Margam. Note that the leading '37' carries the four-black-diamonds logo of the Coal sector of Railfreight. *E. J. Dew/GD*

HEREFORD (2): Barrs Court was an impressive station with two through lines within the station as well as avoiding lines 'around the back'. Looking north on 18 May 1957 there is a fair amount of activity in the station, no doubt to the satisfaction of the train-spotters at the end of the far platform. Indeed, on the near platform one young lad is having a very good look at the footplate of '43XX' Class 2-6-0 No 5377 which is running tender to tender with an unidentified 'Hall'. Waiting in the centre road is BR 'Standard' Class 4-6-0 No 75021.

Except for some cosmetic changes to the footbridge and the removal of the foreground sidings, the area has changed little. The main station building remains as impressive as ever and the train service continues to be buoyant. On 12 October 1992 the 10.04 Manchester Piccadilly to Cardiff Regional Railways service departs formed by Class '158' two-car set No 158817. Behind it two Class '37s' occupy the centre road with the Dee Marsh-Margam steel empties, which will follow the Cardiff train south. *E. J. Dew/GD*

21

LEOMINSTER: Twelve miles north of Hereford lies Leominster, a border market town of some importance. Its growth can, in part, be attributed to its development as a junction town, with the Kington branch of 1857 being the most important. On the other hand, the line to Bromyard and Worcester, as has already been mentioned, struggled for its very life, taking 36 years to progress from inception to completion in 1897. The line to Tenbury Wells and Bewdley would also have been an influence, which left the 'North and West' to the north of Leominster at Wooferton. Accelerating hard from Leominster on a crisp winter's morning is 'Grange' 4-6-0 No 6847 *Tidmarsh Grange* with a southbound goods. The station and signal box are just visible in the background, as is the goods shed on the left. Note the frost on the roof of the coach and the wagons in the goods yard.

A plain double track is all that remains of the extensive railway layout. The station remains open but is unstaffed, while a modern factory unit stands on the site of the goods yard. Heading south is Class '158' No 158839 with the 13.04 Manchester Piccadilly to Cardiff train on 12 October 1992. *Ellis James-Robertson/JW*

ST DEVEREUX: A feature of the 'North and West' line south of Hereford was a string of small wayside stations which served primarily a widespread rural community. St Devereux was a classic example, located 9 miles south of Hereford and at the time of the Grouping served by around five trains daily each way. The station house is lost behind the exhaust of 'Castle' No 5095 *Banbury Castle* which is speeding south with the 1.44 pm Hereford to Cardiff. Note that the station lighting does not appear to have any bulbs or mantles. The station drive is to the right.

The station closed in 1958 along with the neighbouring stations at Pontrilas and Tram Inn. The platforms have been removed but the station house remains, now in private hands. A recent roof extension has been completed and the drive is occupied in part by the garden. Heading south on 17 October 1992 is Class '158' No 158864 with a Manchester to Cardiff train. *Michael Mensing/JW*

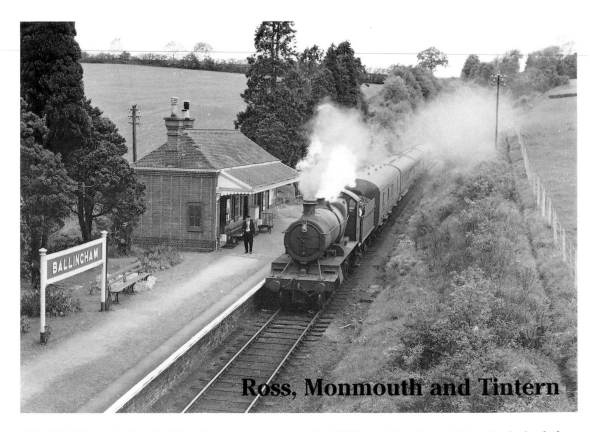

## Ross, Monmouth and Tintern

BALLINGHAM, on the Hereford-Ross line, was perhaps a typical GWR wayside halt consisting of a single platform and booking office. As with many such halts, it was situated some distance from the place it served; indeed, the hamlet of Carey was closer. On 20 May 1964 Class '43XX' 2-6-0 No 7319 calls with a Hereford to Gloucester train. The pristine appearance of the station gives little indication that closure was only six months away. In earlier days this line was used by the GWR as a pilot scheme to perfect techniques for its gauge conversion programme.

Since closure the station premises have passed to private ownership, and although the building has acquired an additional storey, the base is unmistakably the original booking hall. Note also that the platform has survived and now exists as part of the garden. *Hugh Ballantyne/JW*

ROSS-ON-WYE: After several abortive attempts, Ross finally joined the railway age on 1 June 1855 when the Hereford, Ross & Gloucester Railway opened for business. The line was equally important for passenger and freight traffic, as well as being a diversionary route for express trains when the Severn Tunnel was closed. The station was modernised in 1892, which included the provision of a single-storey building, with twin turrets capped with ornate ironwork. Many years later the design was to be recreated by the Severn Valley Railway with its new station at Kidderminster. Ross prospered in the early years, benefitting further when the Ross & Monmouth Railway opened in 1873. On 3 January 1959 ex-GWR '5101' Class 2-6-2T No 5177 approaches with the 10.25 Hereford to Gloucester train. Note the station nameboard: renaming as Ross-on-Wye had officially taken place in 1933, but by the date of this picture the Monmouth line was only two days from closure.

The goods shed survives today, but the remainder of the station site has been obliterated and is now an industrial estate. The station closed in 1964 upon the withdrawal of rail services to the town. *Hugh Ballantyne/JW*

ROSS-ON-WYE ENGINE SHED stood at the eastern end of the station, situated between the Gloucester line (left) and that to Monmouth. Built in 1871, its allocation seemed to fluctuate between three and five locomotives at any one time. Far larger than this photograph would suggest, the single-road shed measured 91 ft long by 20 ft wide, and once boasted a 44 ft turntable at the front. Ross was a sub-shed to Hereford, whose 85C plate is carried by 0-6-0PT No 4657 in June 1957.

The engine shed survives today, now in industrial use. The foreground area which contained the junction has been cleared and is part of an industrial estate with a new road traversing the location. Note that the right-hand houses have changed little, except for the screen of trees. *W. Potter/GD*

KERNE BRIDGE is located where the wide flood plain of the River Wye narrows into a twisting forested gorge to the north of Monmouth. The station took its name from the nearby toll bridge which was one of only two road crossing points between Ross and Monmouth. The first of two railway bridges over the Wye was also situated just to the south of Kerne Bridge station, whilst the river itself can be seen behind the station building in this August 1965 scene. The station, although in good condition, had by this time been closed for six years. Following the withdrawal of passenger services the crossing loop was lifted, although part of the trackwork is still visible just beyond the brake-van. The train is a Lydbrook Junction to Ross goods, hauled by 0-6-0PT No 3775. Note the drainage points set along the platform face as a precaution against flooding.

The B4228 road from Ross has now encroached slightly after being widened, but the station building remains intact and is utilised as an activity centre. Note that part of the old platform also remains in situ in front of the building. *W. Potter/GD*

SYMONDS YAT is located nearly 5 miles north of Monmouth in a picturesque part of the Wye valley. The station was next to the river and became a popular destination for tourists and anglers. By July 1957 the loop had been partially lifted and the remaining stub occupied by a camping coach. A Monmouth to Ross two-coach auto-train, propelled by 0-4-2T No 1455, pauses at the station. Note the attractive wooden station building (left) and the basic wooden shelter on the disused platform (right).

The space between the two platforms has now been filled in, with the whole station area being utilised by the local hotel as a car park. Note the old platform edging slabs just visible to the immediate left of the hotel signboard. *W. Potter/GD*

MONMOUTH TROY: It is difficult to believe that two days after this photograph was taken on 3 January 1959, passenger services to Chepstow and Ross-on-Wye were withdrawn and the station closed. On the right is the 11.00 am from Ross worked by '14XX' 0-4-2T No 1455, whilst on the left is '57XX' No 7774 with the Chepstow and Severn Tunnel Junction service. A further pannier Tank No 7712 is employed in the still busy goods yard. Beyond the station can be seen the junction, with the Ross-on-Wye line diverging to the left over the girder bridge, beyond which was Monmouth's second station, May Hill. To the right, crossing the River Wye by a viaduct, is the Chepstow line. Earlier closures had been to Coleford in 1916, and south towards the main 'North and West' line via Raglan and Usk in 1955.

The course of the railway is still evident today, with the branches to Ross-on-Wye and Chepstow clearly identified by the bridges. The station site has recently been cleared: after years of dereliction, the station building itself has been dismantled brick by brick and transferred to the Gloucestershire & Warwickshire Railway, where it has been reassembled at their Winchcombe station. *Hugh Ballantyne/JW*

TINTERN was perhaps the best known of the four stations on the 14³/₄-mile line from Chepstow (Wye Valley Junction) to Monmouth Troy. The area became a popular tourist attraction due to both the scenery and the nearby ruins of Tintern Abbey, with the station being situated roughly 1 mile to the north of the town. The railway hugged the banks of the River Wye for most of the route, crossing from the east to the west bank at Tintern, and back to the east bank beyond Redbrook. This was a very picturesque line, as for most part both river and railway were tightly hemmed in by the steep wooded slopes. Passenger services were withdrawn on 5 January 1959, and freight in 1964. A short spur remained at the southern end serving Tidenham Quarry until 1990. Two days before the withdrawal of the passenger service, '57XX' No 7774 stands in Tintern with the well-filled 11.50 am from Monmouth Troy to Severn Tunnel Junction.

Upon closure the track was lifted and part of the route was converted into a walkway, utilising the station buildings as a recreational and refreshment centre. The signal box also remains, but the island platform has been removed. The railway presence is retained by virtue of two preserved passenger coaches on a short length of standard gauge track together with a miniature railway. *Hugh Ballantyne/JW*

# Chepstow and Severn bridges

WYE BRIDGE, CHEPSTOW: The South Wales Railway opened between Swansea and Chepstow in June 1850, and from Gloucester to Chepstow in September 1851. It did not become a through route until July 1852 when the 'gap' was filled by the opening of Brunel's bridge over the River Wye at Chepstow. It was a tubular suspension bridge with two towers 150 feet above low water level. Whilst not the most attractive of designs, Brunel put the lessons learned at Chepstow to good use in his famous Royal Albert Bridge over the Tamar at Saltash, completed in 1859. Wye Bridge remained in its original form until 1962 when it was rebuilt with the train deck supported from below by a lattice girder arrangement. The reconstructed bridge is well illustrated in this April 1980 scene showing Class '47' No 47512 heading north with the 11.45 Cardiff-Newcastle Inter-City service.

Further change has since taken place, resulting in this wider viewpoint: the rail bridge remains unaltered but alongside is now positioned the new road bridge which carries the main A48 Gloucester road clear of Chepstow's winding streets. The steepness of the valley here is also well illustrated. Crossing the rail bridge is Class '47' No 47803 heading Regional Railways' 10.50 Cardiff-Nottingham service on 12 October 1992. The locomotive and stock are on hire from Inter-City due to problems with the new Class '158' DMUs which normally operate this service. *Brian Morrison/JW*

SEVERN RAILWAY BRIDGE: The fate of the Severn Railway Bridge, and the Sharpness to Lydney line which used it, was sealed on the foggy night of 25 October 1960 when the 229-ton petrol tanker *Wastdale* collided with it and demolished two spans. Five lives were lost in the accident, but the loss could have been far greater as a train had crossed the bridge only minutes earlier. The Severn Railway Bridge had opened in 1872 but was secondary to the Severn Tunnel which opened in 1886; while the former dealt mainly with local traffic and was single track, the latter was built at a strategically key position on a main line with double track. Through freight diversions used the bridge when the tunnel was closed as an alternative to the usual route via Gloucester. This is the scene at Severn Bridge station on 6 August 1961, ten months after the accident; all the railway infrastructure remains in place except that access to the bridge is barred by a fence between the stone abutments, and the two missing spans are clearly evident. The Gloucester to South Wales main line runs beneath the stone piers leading to the bridge, and

at the far end the white control room of the swing bridge section can be seen. The swing bridge spanned the Gloucester and Sharpness Canal.

The bridge was demolished completely by 1970 and, except for the lifting of the tracks, Severn Bridge station appears to have been left to rot quietly. The platforms remain in situ, as does, amazingly, the signal box which has now been repossessed by nature in the same way that the jungle would take over a long-deserted colonial mansion! This view looks over the Severn from the remains of the eastbound platform towards the void where the bridge once stood. *C. G. Maggs/JW*

# Forest of Dean

LYDNEY ENGINE SHED: On 7 August 1957 a trio of 0-6-0PTs simmer outside the three-road shed at Lydney, whilst a '43XX' 2-6-0 is visible within the running shed itself. Lydney was a sub-shed to Gloucester (85B) and serviced the requirements of the Forest of Dean system. It dated back to 1865, being rebuilt in 1876 and further enlarged to its maximum size in 1891. To the left is the repair shop, and the general stores are on the far right. The coaling stage is left of centre and once boasted a crane. Note the inspection pits beneath the left-hand wagon and the pannier tank parked next to the coaling stage.

The site today is used for heavy goods vehicles, perhaps reflecting the changed priorities and preferences over the years. Note, though, the Dean Forest Preservation Society's line running in the foreground. (See also page 6) *W. Potter/GD*

PARKEND: On 6 August 1965 ex-GW '57XX' 0-6-0 No 4698 shunts coal wagons at Marsh Sidings at Parkend; the train is about to cross the main Lydney to Cinderford road. To the right are wagons of domestic coal stabled in the station yard, whilst the black wooden building (extreme right) is the goods shed and dates back to the beginning of this century. Parkend was an early important industrial centre served by tramways until the arrival of the railway in 1868. The passenger station is beyond the right-hand coal wagons and doubles also as the junction station for the nearby Coleford branch.

The course of Marsh Sidings remains clearly evident with rail still in situ as far as the main road. The area beyond also appears to have changed remarkably little, with even the now ancient goods shed still in place, albeit boarded up. Missing today is the bus shelter, but the Mini car, seen on the left of the 'past' scene, can still be purchased new today, some 27 years later - some motor-car! *W. Potter/GD*

PARKEND GOODS: Marsh Sidings followed the course of the Milkwall Tramway, which was abandoned in 1876, whilst the sidings survived into the diesel era of British Railways. On 10 June 1968 Class '22' diesel-hydraulic No D6319 shunts ballast wagons. After the closure of the Coleford branch, ballast was transported from Whitecliff Quarry by road to Marsh Sidings. The line on the left was used to load coal from several private mines for movement to Newport Power Station. The Milkwall Tramway was located on the right and the Oakwood Tramway terminated at the loading wharf.

The area has now been completely levelled and only the right-hand wall and background buildings, which appear to have changed little, identify the location. *W. Potter/GD*

TRAVELLERS REST CROSSING took its name from a nearby, but long-closed, public house of the same name. Situated on the Coleford to Blakeney Road, the signal box not only controlled the road crossing but also served as a block post between Parkend and Coleford Junction. On 6 August 1965 0-6-0PT No 4698 heads south with a consist of ballast from Whitecliff Quarry and empty domestic coal wagons from Coleford. Although by this time long closed, a siding once ran behind the signal box to Parkend Colliery, and a stoneworks was located roughly to the right of the bracket home signal in the background.

Today the location has drastically changed, with only the left-hand fence surviving from the earlier scene. Note that on the right the roadway is elevated above the old trackbeds, and probably follows the course of the old colliery siding. *W. Potter/GD*

MILKWALL: The branch to Coleford opened in 1875, utilising in part the Milkwall Tramway. The only intermediate station was located at Milkwall, which consisted of a single platform and loop. The original wooden station building survived until 1923, when it was destroyed by fire. A more substantial brick and tile structure was then provided, which became the goods office after the cessation of the passenger services in 1929. Goods services were operated both to Coleford and on to the Sling branch, the latter joining the main line at Milkwall. On 18 August 1965 0-6-0PT No 4698 prepares to propel a train destined for Watkins Boiler Works along the branch.

Today's view is taken from a wider vantage point. The course of the Sling branch recedes in the centre whilst to the right is the remains of the distinctive Easter Iron Mines engine house. Note that the right-hand corrugated iron workshop also remains, but the neighbouring unit has had its distinctive curved roof replaced by a more traditional gable. *W. Potter/GD*

SLING BRANCH: Later on the same day, 18 August 1965, 0-6-0PT No 4698 shunts the siding at the British Mining and Colour Works, situated on the branch at Milkwall. Note the chimney on the extreme right which stands on the semi-derelict house that can be seen left of centre in the Milkwall station photograph opposite. An idea of the stiff gradient at this location can be obtained by noting how the railway dips towards Milkwall station while the main road climbs away in the distance. As a consequence it was usual for trains to be propelled along the branch to avoid wagon runaways.

The main part of the old Colour Works remains today, with the only real change being the provision of the new foreground building in place of the loading bay. It would also appear that the course of the railway has been filled in, as there is no trace of the actual platform. In the background the houses remain distinctive, but the property at the extreme right appears to have either been extended or replaced. *W. Potter/GD*

SLING BRANCH, SAND SIDING: Another scene from 18 August 1965, as No 4698 again works the branch, conveying scrap metal from Watkins Boiler Works. The train is passing Sand Siding, a short spur off the 52-chain branch. An inscription on the point lever suggested that the siding dated back to 1878, and probably existed to cater for a nearby sand quarry. In order to use the siding the 'locomotive to propel' rule had to be ignored, although there appears to be little to restrain any wagons deposited in the siding.

The caravan park in the 1965 scene has now given way to more permanent residences, whilst the background trees have grown considerably. The location can be confirmed by the electricity pylons, whose position today pinpoints the course of the railway. Note the street lighting bracket which has also survived, albeit with a different light globe. *W. Potter/GD*

COLEFORD JUNCTION: A busy scene at Coleford Junction on 18 June 1965 as 0-6-0PT No 4698 arrives with the first train of the day from Gloucester and Lydney. It has domestic coal for Coleford (Severn & Wye) station and empty ballast hoppers for Whitecliff Quarry. Note the wagons on the left, loaded with round tanks, which are from Watkins Boiler Works located on the Sling Branch. To reach Coleford a reversal was necessary; the branch can be seen diverging to the right beyond the rear of the train. Passenger trains divided here, with the Cinderford portion continuing north whilst the branch engine would collect the usual two coaches for Coleford (GW). A workman's platform was located roughly at the point from which this photograph was taken, but lasted for only a short time and had been removed by the turn of the century. The signal box dates back to 1925 when the GWR pattern replaced the original Severn & Wye structure.

The entire site today has been cleared, with no trace of the railway remaining. The background caravans mark the point roughly where the Coleford branch diverged. *W. Potter/GD*

COLEFORD (GW): On 16 August 1965 0-6-0PT No 4698 simmers in Coleford (GW) whilst the crew enjoy a well-earned break. The train consists of one empty wagon for Whitecliff Quarry plus a brake van. The Great Western station dated from 1883, when the line from Monmouth reached the town, but the passenger service was of short duration, being withdrawn in 1916. The Severn & Wye Railway had reached Coleford eight years earlier in 1875, with the passenger service via Coleford Junction surviving until 1929. Whilst in close proximity, interchange between the stations was problematical, initially due to the intense rivalry between the two companies. Operational difficulties remained until 1951 when a new layout was installed which enabled through running on to the stub of the old Great Western Monmouth line, allowing easier access for trains to Whitecliff Quarry. The building on the right is the original Great Western goods shed.

Although the site today is occupied by a supermarket, one corner remains dedicated to the railway. The Great Western Railway Museum is housed in the old 1883 GW goods shed and features the railways of the Forest of Dean. Amongst items of rolling-stock is a Pecket 0-4-0 tank locomotive and a full-size ex-GW signal box which last stood on the busy West of England main line at Cogload Junction, north of Taunton. The museum, which opened in 1988, contains a wealth of information on the local railways and appeals to the general and specialist enthusiast alike. *W. Potter/GD*

WHITECLIFF QUARRY: Whitecliff Quarry stood on the remains of the ex-Great Western line from Monmouth to Coleford, which closed in 1916. The quarry was located some 17 chains from Coleford, with a short tunnel the only major engineering feature, access being by way of a ground frame. On 31 May 1966 a Class '14' 650 hp diesel-hydraulic locomotive shunts hopper wagons within the complex.

The scene is now one of dereliction and destruction: on the hillside (right) can be seen the remains of the conveyor supports whilst the barren foreground once contained the sidings and the main buildings. The quarry itself closed in 1967. *W. Potter/GD*

**BRADLEY HILL TUNNEL:** The Great Western branch to Cinderford diverged from the South Wales main line at Bullo Pill, whose harbour for a time competed with Lydney for the river trade. The branch had a difficult and curvaceous route with the need for three tunnels, one such being at Bradley Hill. On 11 October 1965 0-6-0PT No 3675 emerges under full power from the tunnel with a train of empties for Northern United Colliery. On the far left can be seen the stop block and platform which once served a short siding. Contemporary photographs taken at this point indicate that the siding had been removed within the previous 12 months.

The narrow bore of Bradley Hill Tunnel can be seen in the background of the present-day view, now bricked up. The house shows little change whilst the course of the railway remains evident. A metalled road now crosses the site, following in part the bed of the old siding. *W. Potter/GD*

SOUDLEY: A classic branch-line scene at Soudley as 0-6-0PT No 4689 drifts past with a southbound goods comprised mainly of wagons from the Rosedale Plastic Factory at Cinderford. Remains of the long-closed station are plainly evident, with the platform facing still in position. An idea of the steepness of the valley can be gained by noting that the chimneys of the left-hand properties are below the railway whilst the gable roof of the White Horse Inn (behind the locomotive) occupies a much higher vantage point.

The surrounding area has changed little in the intervening years, with the course of the railway still intact. Note that part of the old platform face remains and that the distinctive tree (centre) continues to flourish. *W. Potter/GD*

**STAPLE EDGE HALT:** A train of gas tar tanks from the Tarmacadam Works at Whimsey approaches the site of Staple Edge Halt, hauled by 0-6-0PT No 9672. To the left of the train is the remains of a siding which once connected the now closed Eastern United Colliery to the main line; note the derelict mine buildings on the far left-hand side.

An industrial unit occupies part of the site today, but note how the conifer tree (centre) has matured over the years from the rather thinner specimen situated to the right of the locomotive's cab in the earlier view. This location is to the south of Ruspidge and close to Blue Rock Tunnel, one of the three major engineering features on this part of the line. *W. Potter/GD*

RUSPIDGE: Although a halt, Ruspidge was the nearest that the Great Western got to Cinderford until its spur from Bilson Junction was opened in 1908; consequently the buildings have more substance than the traditional halt. On 26 September 1965 0-6-0PT No 4698 heads a southbound train from Northern United Colliery, watched by the crossing keeper. The foreground contains a wealth of railway infrastructure with single-span crossing gates and ornate cast lamp-posts being a feature.

Today the location of the railway can still be clearly seen, as can Cinderford in the background. A remaining feature is the power cable pylons which clearly locate the scene today. *W. Potter/GD*

BILSON JUNCTION was situated at the southern end of a web of lines where the old Severn & Wye system met the Great Western near Cinderford. Four separate lines are featured in this September 1965 view: on the extreme right is the spur constructed in 1908 which enabled the Great Western to reach Cinderford Town, whilst beyond that, curving to the right just in front of the background trees, is the line to Whimsey. Ahead, beyond the raft of mineral wagons, is the branch to Churchway, on which stood the Northern United Colliery, whilst crossing on an embankment just behind the wagons is the Severn & Wye line from Drybrook. The signal box is of standard Great Western design, as is the traction in the form of 0-6-0PT No 4689 heading tank wagons from the Tarmacadam Works at Whimsey. Although the tracks to Churchway and Whimsey appear a little unkept, the Cinderford spur is well maintained, which gives the whole scene a timeless atmosphere. In fact, closure was less than two years away.

The lie of the background hills is the best pointer to the location today, as no trace of the railway remains. The mound (left of centre) roughly corresponds to where the wagons were stabled. *W. Potter/GD*

CINDERFORD: Some four months prior to complete closure, Cinderford Town station remains remarkably intact as BR Type 1 diesel-hydraulic No 9503 shunts the daily goods in April 1967. The station, which dated from July 1900 and replaced the original and inconveniently located Severn & Wye facility, still retains its canopy, whilst the goods shed shows signs of activity. Originally planned by the Severn & Wye, the station was actually built by the succeeding joint Midland & Great Western Railway Company. It was not until 1908, with the completion of the spur from Bilson Junction, that the Great Western actually obtained access, thus enabling through running from Newnham and eventually Gloucester.

A housing estate occupies the site today, with BMWs and Vauxhalls replacing Panniers and Prairies! The background does retain some familiar features, however, with the gabled public house and factory remaining. *W. Potter/GD*

# Ashchurch and branches

ASHCHURCH was important due to its junction status: on the left is the branch to Malvern via Upton-upon-Severn and Tewkesbury, and on the right the line to Evesham and Redditch, the so-called 'Birmingham Loop'. On a warm July day in 1959 both branch-line trains await departure: the Upton service is in the hands of an ex-MR 0-4-4T with a single coach whilst a Class '2P' 4-4-0 is in charge of the five-coach 'Loop' line train. The station is of classic Midland design, with typical gabled wrought iron and glass canopies. The well at the end of the up platform is where the original signal box stood, having been replaced by a more modern structure off the picture to the right. A serious accident occurred here on 8 January 1929 when a Bristol to Leeds express overran signals.

Ashchurch closed in 1971 and the scene today reveals much rationalisation, with the branch towards Tewkesbury having disappeared completely. To the right, above Class '156' 'Sprinter' No 156413 which forms a Birmingham to Cardiff service, can be seen the remains of the Evesham line, which until recently served Ashchurch MoD depot, whilst in the foreground the goods platform and part of the fence remain intact. Note the distinctive tree, which reveals the site of the main line and Evesham branch platform. *Peter Shoesmith/GD*

ECKINGTON: Just under 5 miles north of Ashchurch is Eckington, one of four intermediate stations between Ashchurch and Worcester. It was served primarily by local trains and its closure in 1965 was a result of the withdrawal of the stopping services on the route. The station had a distinctive building, almost chapel-like in appearance. At the northern end on the down side stood the Midland pattern signal box which guarded the level crossing. On 7 August 1956 Class '4F' 0-6-0 No 44591 heads a southbound unfitted freight.

Today the station building has survived, although the vestibule has been removed. The platforms, signal box and level crossing have all gone, with a modern footbridge preserving the pedestrian right of way. Approaching is a southbound HST. *Peter Shoesmith/B. M. Williams*

BECKFORD: The Birmingham and Gloucester 'Loop' was primarily a rural railway, the only major towns *en route* being Redditch and Evesham. It served the eastern flank of Worcestershire and owed its existence to pressure from the local farming community and Redditch industrialists for an efficient means to transport their produce to market, as the main line via the Lickey Incline was simply too far away. Completion was in 1868, with Beckford being the most southerly station situated 4 miles from Ashchurch. The station buildings, and particularly the nameboard, indicate the Midland origins of the line as ex-GW 0-6-0PT No 3745 calls on 15 June 1963. This was to be the last scheduled passenger train on the line, with freight services remaining for a further year.

The scene has now altered considerably, but closer inspection reveals that the station house (extreme right) and goods shed remain. Also note how the trackbed has been put to good use as a sunken garden and pond, with the right-hand retaining wall utilising the old platform face. *Michael Mensing/GD*

TEWKESBURY (1): The passenger service from Ashchurch to Tewkesbury commenced in 1840, although it is thought that the branch existed prior to that date for the movement of materials delivered to Tewkesbury by river for the construction of the main line. *Bradshaw* of 1922 indicates nine trains per day each way, taking on average 5 minutes to complete a 1³/₄-mile journey between the two stations. On 4 July 1959 push-pull fitted Class '2P' 0-4-4T No 41900 awaits departure for Ashchurch.

It is difficult to locate the site of the station today, as demolition took place after closure in 1964, and nature has taken over. The rather flatter ground running from the centre to the bottom right-hand corner indicates the platform location, with the trackbed beyond recognisable only due to being at a lower level. *Peter Shoesmith/JW*

TEWKESBURY (2): The engine shed at Tewkesbury came under the control of Gloucester Depot (22B), and was located at the end of a spur which ran from the station towards the town centre via a goods yard. On 21 May 1956 Stanier Class '5' 4-6-0 No 44965 is being serviced, whilst in the background on the left stands a Class '4F' 0-6-0 and on the right a Class '3F' 0-6-0.

A car park now stands on the site of the engine shed, but the distinctive buildings both to the centre and on the left clearly pinpoint the location today. *Peter Shoesmith/JW*

NEAR RIPPLE: Beyond Tewkesbury the branch continued northwards towards Upton-upon-Severn and Malvern Wells, where it connected with the Worcester to Hereford main line. The construction of the M50 necessitated a new bridge to carry both railway and road over the new motorway at a point just south of Ripple; the motorway is just visible here in the bottom left-hand corner as 0-6-0PT No 7788 heads north with an Upton-upon-Severn service in the summer of 1961.

The scene today shows little change except for the lifting of the railway. The trackbed is intact, as is the bridge with its girders still in good condition. *Ellis James-Robertson/JW*

RIPPLE is no more than a village located between Upton-upon-Severn and Tewkesbury, but despite its size it enjoyed the facilities of a quite impressive station. On 4 July 1959 Class '2P' 0-4-4T No 41900 approaches with an Ashchurch-bound service. The line north of Tewkesbury did not boast a frequent passenger service, having only four trains per day each way just prior to 1923 when the Grouping of the railway companies took place. Through trains from Ashchurch to Malvern Link were the first casualty in 1952, with the Upton-upon-Severn service being lost in 1961, whilst trains to Tewkesbury survived until 1964.

Miraculously, upon closure in 1961 the buildings were not demolished and have since been purchased for use as a private residence. Although considerable renovation has taken place, the character of the buildings has not changed and the glory that was once Ripple railway station remains. *Peter Shoesmith/JW (courtesy of Mr & Mrs Fullerlove)*

# GW lines to Cheltenham

LAVERTON: The Cheltenham to Honeybourne line was engineered by the Great Western to connect with its North Warwickshire Line and provide a through route to Birmingham, freeing it from having to use Midland metals north of Cheltenham. The through route opened in 1908 but the price of independence was a longer way round than the Midland route via the Lickey Incline. South of Honeybourne the Great Western route served mainly rural communities with a dozen intermediate stations or halts. The village of Laverton, the location of one such halt, is roughly 1 mile north of this scene showing 'Grange' 4-6-0 No 6846 *Ruckley Grange* heading a northbound Sunday engineering train attending to lineside telegraph poles.

The abutments and retaining wall of the A46 road over-bridge remain in good condition today, and while the track has long been lifted, the course of the railway is still clearly evident. Hopefully in the not too distant future trains will again pass this way, but this time courtesy of the Gloucester & Warwickshire Steam Railway.
*Michael Mensing/JW*

TODDINGTON was an important centre on the route with an impressive passenger station and substantial goods yard which was kept busy catering for the local fruit-growing industry. On 27 February 1960 a Swindon 'Cross-Country' DMU calls at Toddington with the 12.25 Birmingham Snow Hill to Carmarthen train. Local services were withdrawn one week later, and the station was closed, although a through service, together with parcels and freight traffic, survived until March 1968. In latter days the only intermediate signal box was sited at Toddington which was adequate for the dwindling traffic. Effective closure occurred on 15 August 1976 when a freight train derailment south of the station caused extensive track damage.

Between the dates of these two views the station became derelict and the platforms were bulldozed away. However, on the closure of the line the Gloucestershire & Warwickshire Steam Railway was formed, and by 1981 had purchased the trackbed and ultimately recreated this splendid scene today. Presently running an hourly service between Toddington and Gretton Halt, a further $1^{1}/_{4}$ miles to Bishop Cleeve is due to open in 1993. The Railway's ultimate aim is to reach Cheltenham Racecourse by 1999 before turning north towards Broadway - an exciting prospect for a friendly and ambitious railway that is well worth a visit. *Hugh Ballantyne/JW*

CHELTENHAM ST JAMES'S station was located at the end of a 1¹/₄-mile spur from the Birmingham-Bristol main line at Cheltenham Lansdown. It originally served Great Western trains from the Swindon line, and later Banbury and Southampton services, as well as some trains off the Honeybourne route. The best-known train using St James's was the 'Cheltenham Flyer' which in the 1930s was the world's fastest steam train. The major advantage that St James's enjoyed over Lansdown was its position close to the town centre, giving passengers easy access to all the shops and other facilities. Decline came quickly, however, as train services were either withdrawn or diverted, and closure took place on 3 January 1966.

The station site has been cleared and is now used as a car park. Remaining as a distinctive feature on the left is the spire of the Church of St Gregory the Great alongside which now stand the offices of Mercantile and General Re-Insurance. *C. G. Maggs/JW*

CHELTENHAM MALVERN ROAD: The line to Honeybourne was built from the existing spur to St James's and upon completion in 1908 was served by a new station at Malvern Road, which was sited roughly mid-way between Lansdown and St James's. Malvern Road provided the Great Western with a second outlet in Cheltenham, and it grew in importance when the GWR was able to transfer its West of England traffic to the new through route. Malvern Road had a life span of only 58 years, however, closing on 3 January 1966 along with St James's. This view is from the west end and was taken during the late 1950s as a first-generation Swindon-built 'Inter City' DMU passes with a southbound train. Malvern Road engine shed is prominent in the background, in front of which is a well-stocked goods yard. 'Cheltenham Spa Malvern Road West Signal Box' is on the left and must be a candidate for having one of the GWR's longest name-boards!

The station has long been demolished, and a public footpath now follows the course of the railway. A DIY store and builders yard occupies the site of the goods yard and shed. Note the house situated on the extreme right of the DIY store, which can also be seen between the engine shed and signal post in the earlier photograph. *Peter Shoesmith/GD*

CHARLTON KINGS: On 27 February 1960 '5101' Class 'Prairie' 2-6-2T No 4116 eases into Charlton Kings with the 11.18 am Kingham to Cheltenham (St James's) service. The halt, which was situated on the southern outskirts of Cheltenham, survived until 1962, when the passenger service was withdrawn. Note, however, that the main station building was already boarded up, although generally the location seems to be in reasonable condition. This route, which was completed in 1887, was a scenic cross-country route linking Cheltenham to Banbury.

The site today has been levelled and is occupied by a modern factory estate. The distinctive road bridge remains, however, as does the attractive gabled house on the far left-hand side. *Hugh Ballantyne/GD*

ANDOVERSFORD JUNCTION: Seven miles from Cheltenham was Andoversford Junction, so called because it was the point at which the Midland & South Western Junction line to Cirencester, Swindon and the South Coast diverged from the Banbury line. This through route was completed in 1891, with running powers over Great Western metals from Andoversford to Cheltenham. The passenger service had variable fortunes, but particularly during the war years the line was of considerable strategic value as a through route from the industrial Midlands to the South Coast. As an independent company it was always in competition with the Great Western, with four through services each way just prior to the Grouping. On 7 September 1955, Class '43XX' 2-6-0 No 6387 drifts into the Junction Station (GW) with the 2.00 pm Cheltenham (St James's) to Southampton train. The rival Andoversford & Dowdeswell station (M&SWJ) had closed in 1927, while the through route itself survived until 1961.

A scene of total dereliction marks the location today with only the platform edge (right centre bottom) giving an indication of the railway's former presence. *Hugh Ballantyne/GD*

BOURTON-ON-THE-WATER: The through route from Cheltenham to Banbury was actually achieved in three stages, with the opening in 1862 of 6¹/₂ miles from Chipping Norton Junction (later Kingham) to Bourton-on-the Water being the second stage; the connection with Cheltenham was not completed until 1881. Bourton-on-the-Water became a tourist attraction, and the station boasted a crossing loop. On 29 September 1962, with closure imminent, Class '5101' 'Prairie' 2-6-2T No 5184 departs with the 10.50 am Cheltenham (St James's) to Kingham, whilst another 'Prairie', No 4101, heads the 11.18 am from Kingham. To the left, beyond the wagon, is sited a goods shed. Amazingly, although the site is being redeveloped with modern housing, the station buildings remain, complete with canopy. A road now covers the actual line, and the road overbridge at the Cheltenham end has been removed. *Hugh Ballantyne/GD*

Gloucester

GLOUCESTER CENTRAL: The Central station of today stands on the site of the original Gloucester stations of the Birmingham & Gloucester and South Wales railways, and was inherited by the Great Western, while the Midland later moved to Eastgate. The station had all the trappings of a Great Western building, being of traditional design - note the ornate ironwork cresting the roof line to the right of the footbridge. Passing through the centre road is '56XX' Class 0-6-2T No 6631 with an eastbound freight in June 1956. The locomotive is a development of an earlier Collett design introduced in 1924 specifically for working the steeply graded South Wales Valley lines.

In 1975 Central again became the main station when Eastgate closed. Because the Tuffley loop through Eastgate has also closed, trains visiting Gloucester on the Birmingham-Bristol axis are now required once more to reverse direction in the station. To improve operating flexibility a 608-yard platform was constructed which can accommodate two trains. To further improve operations the old parcels platforms were reopened to passenger traffic and a new footbridge installed. On 3 July 1986 Class '47' No 47549 *Royal Mail* is re-attached after running round the 11.00 Liverpool-Plymouth express, and will soon be heading south-westwards once more. *Norman Preedy/JW*

GLOUCESTER EASTGATE opened in 1896 enabling Midland trains to have through running between Birmingham and Bristol, thus avoiding the inconvenient run-round required in the old station. Its platforms were sharply curved, as can be seen in this June 1957 view as ex-LMS 'Jubilee' 4-6-0 No 45654 *Hood* restarts the 'Devonian' express, which ran from Bradford to Kingswear. A long footbridge connected Eastgate and Central stations which was a cause of considerable inconvenience, especially to passengers with any quantity of luggage. Eastgate closed in 1975 along with the Tuffley loop, and all services were again concentrated on Central station.

A by-pass and supermarket now occupy the site of Eastgate. The road curves in from the left, following in part the direction of the old station connecting footbridge. The supermarket actually straddles the station site as can be judged by the building (far right) which has survived re-development. *Norman Preedy/JW*

BARTON STREET LEVEL CROSSING was situated just beyond the south end of Eastgate station and was one of five on the Tuffley loop. In later years these crossings were a considerable cause of traffic chaos, which was an influencing factor in the loop being eventually closed. The distinctive signal box straddled both track and roadway and carried the name 'Barton Street Junction'. On 1 June 1963 'Jubilee' 4-6-0 No 45685 *Barfleur* has charge of a Wolverhampton to Paignton express. The locomotive has cleared the crossing and Eastgate is just visible in the distance.

The church (extreme right) is all that remains of the scene today, as a dual-carriageway road now obliterates the course of the railway. Traffic jams are still a feature but now sheer volume of traffic causes the problems! *Norman Preedy/JW*

HIGH ORCHARD BRANCH (1): The importance of Gloucester Docks grew during the early 19th century, eventually being served by branches from both the Midland and Great Western railways. The Midland branch was called High Orchard, and it left the main line at Barton Street Junction. On 21 November 1970 a Metropolitan-Cammell three-car DMU visited the branch with a railtour from Birmingham, and is seen passing California Crossing signal box; the main line from Eastgate is hidden from view by the wall. The branch then skirted Gloucester Recreational Park before reaching the docks.

The High Orchard tracks have long since disappeared, having been closed completely in 1971. Note the row of houses (far right) which serves to pinpoint the course of the old main line, the turn off on the right being the location of California Crossing. *Hugh Ballantyne/JW*

HIGH ORCHARD BRANCH (2): A short freight train is being shunted at High Orchard sidings on 29 March 1963. In charge is ex-Midland Railway Deeley 0-4-0T No 41537, one of two such locomotives (the other being 41535) allocated to Barnwood shed for working into and around the docks. There were only eight members of the class, first introduced in 1907. The docks were situated on the Gloucester & Sharpness Ship Canal and survived until 1989. The Great Western branch from Over Junction served mainly the western side of the complex (Llanthony Dock), although both companies had access to the docks' private railway system.

The factories in the background remain, but the railway sidings have been removed. The centre of the docks complex has been sympathetically restored and is now an attractive recreational complex containing both waterways and packaging museums. The centre also plays host to a number of public events throughout the year. *Norman Preedy/JW*

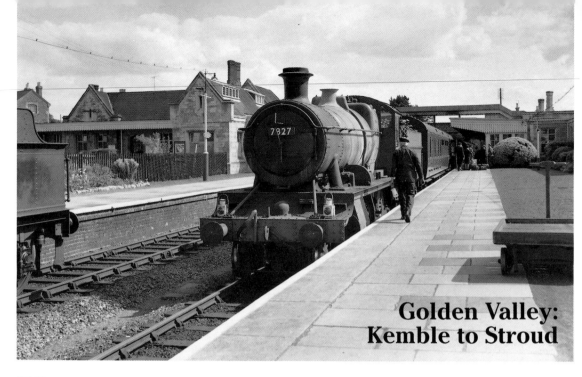

# Golden Valley:
# Kemble to Stroud

KEMBLE: The railway arrived at Kemble in 1841, although for many years development around the station area was inhibited due to the opposition of a local landowner. The present station dates from 1872 and is unusual by virtue of the buildings being at right angles to the track. Originally part of the Cheltenham & Great Western Union Railway which ran from Swindon to Cirencester via Kemble, it passed to Great Western ownership in 1844. The GWR completed the through route from Kemble to Gloucester (in 1845) and Cheltenham (in 1847) at which time Kemble became a junction with the branch to Cirencester (the former main line), and later also a branch to Tetbury, constructed in 1889. On 5 August 1962 ex-Great Western '43XX' 2-6-0 No 7327 awaits departure with the 1.20 pm (Sundays) Paddington to Gloucester.

It is pleasing to note that today Kemble has lost little of its charm, remaining virtually intact. The branches have gone, and the line between Swindon and Kemble has now been singled, but the service remains buoyant. Class '150/2' 'Sprinter' No 150278 departs for Gloucester with a stopping service from Swindon. *Mrs Toni Ballantyne/GD*

CIRENCESTER TOWN: Cirencester temporarily found itself at the northern end of the Cheltenham & Great Western Union Railway's Swindon to Gloucester and Cheltenham main line when first opened in 1841. It was some four years later, when the line was extended from Kemble towards Stroud, that it became a branch line of $4^{1}/_{2}$ miles in length under GWR ownership. Brunel, and his assistant Brereton, designed the impressive Gothic-style Town station which once boasted an overall roof. On 27 September 1958 ex-GWR 0-6-0PT No 9672 can be seen shunting stock in the station yard. During the following years steam gave way to a diesel railbus service, and although there was a quite intensive service of 15 trains per day, it was not sufficiently popular to prevent the complete loss of the passenger service in 1964, at which point the line closed. A second station served the town on the through Midland & South Western line between Swindon, Andoversford and Cheltenham, which closed in 1959.

Today, Town station is the subject of a preservation order and remains in good condition. The building is still connected with transport, now being used as a bus terminus, while the station yard is put to use as a car park. *Peter Shoesmith/GD*

TETBURY: The 7¹/₂-mile branch to Tetbury was completed in 1889. During its existence intermediate stops were at Rodmarton (opened 1904), Jackaments Bridge (1939-1948 for the local RAF base) and Culkerton (closed 1956). When new railbuses were introduced in 1959, Culkerton was reopened and new halts were opened at Church Hill and Trouble House. The railbus experiment was an attempt to operate rural branch lines efficiently and on 7 February 1964 railbus No 79976, one of five lightweight four-wheeled vehicles built by AC Cars Limited, stands at the terminus in Tetbury. A basic eight trains per day pattern existed, with a journey time of approximately 24 minutes. Unfortunately the experiment was not fully successful and the service was withdrawn, closure taking place in April 1964. The station building dated back to 1913, whilst a platform extension later took place to deal with consignments of polo ponies for nearby Beaufort polo park. Beyond the station can be glimpsed the goods shed, which closed in 1963 when freight traffic on the branch was withdrawn, and the single-loco engine shed with integral water tower.

Only the station drive exists today, although the site of the building can be judged by the grassed area, now only of interest to dogs! Note, however, the outline of the distant gable (centre) indicating the survival of the goods shed. *Hugh Ballantyne/GD*

74

FRAMPTON MANSELL VIADUCT: Beyond Kemble the line climbs to Sapperton Tunnel, after which it drops into the Golden Valley. This has always been a favourite location for photographers, particularly as the graceful nine-arch viaduct blends well with the surrounding valley and buildings of local Cotswold stone. It is also the point where up trains are working hard on the climb from Stroud to Sapperton, as evidenced by 'Castle' 4-6-0 No 5071 *Spitfire* head-ing a Cheltenham to Paddington express off the viaduct on 18 October 1958. The 'Castle' Class was first introduced in 1923, but No 5071 was of a batch built in 1938; originally named *Clifford Castle*, it was soon re-named after the wartime aircraft.

The viaduct and valley remain unchanged today, except that the bushes have grown somewhat and now restrict the view. The railway remains a distinctive feature, with most passenger services now in the hands of Regional Railways' new generation of DMUs. On 5 September 1991 Class '155' No 155332 heads west with the 14.20 Swindon to Gloucester train. This type of unit is now being split into single-car units to operate on rural low-density lines. Note that refuge points have been inserted along the parapet wall for the safety of permanent way work-men. *Peter Shoesmith/GD*

CHALFORD: Seven miles west of Kemble is Chalford, an attractive rural station set deep in the densely-wooded valley. In latter years it was the terminus for the auto-train service from Gloucester, and on 6 May 1961 0-4-2T No 1424 is seen arriving with the 10.08 service from that city. Behind the station building is the goods bay, occupied by W189W, one of a batch of 62 ft 8 in bow-end auto-trailers introduced in 1933.

The station was closed in 1964, since when the buildings and platforms have been removed and the area taken over by a building supplies firm. Passing the old station site in autumn 1991 is a Bristol-based DMU with car 56312 leading, which forms the 14.15 Gloucester-Swindon service. *Hugh Ballantyne/B. M. Williams*

BRIMSCOMBE: A fascinating railway scene is evident at Brimscombe on 7 March 1964. The station, footbridge and signal box can be seen in the background, all of typical Great Western pattern, while in the centre is a one-road engine shed with the unusual feature of the water tower forming an integral part of the whole building - this was a useful way of preventing the water from freezing in winter. Standing in front of the shed and taking water is 'Prairie' 2-6-2T No 4109, the duty banker awaiting the next freight to be assisted up to Sapperton, the ruling gradient being 1 in 74. The locomotive carries the shed code of Gloucester (85B), to which Brimscombe was a sub-shed.

With the station and shed gone, the top corner of the block of flats (top right) is the only feature to link the scene today. The station, along with the nearby Brimscombe Bridge Halt, closed in 1964. In the centre can be seen a white building, which is a public house known as the King and Castle; the outline of a locomotive is just visible on the pub sign in front of the building. This view does illustrate the tight confines of the location as Class '155' No 155332 passes with the 11.56 Worcester to Swindon train. *Hugh Ballantyne/B. M. Williams*

STROUD: Of all the intermediate stations, Stroud is by far the most important. Not only was it served by the Great Western, forming part of the original main line to South Wales prior to the building of the Severn Tunnel, but also the Midland, to a separate station at the end of a spur from Dudbridge on the Nailsworth branch (see following pages). The Great Western route was the most important, though, and its station was re-built in 1914 to provide the appropriate facilities for this bustling market town. The approach from the west carried the railway over a substantial viaduct, and to the east, on the up side, was situated a distinctive goods shed and yard. On 26 March 1964 ex-GW 0-4-2T No 1451 departs with the 1.03 pm Gloucester to Chalford auto-train consisting of a single coach. These trains took over from steam railmotors, which had previously operated the service successfully for many years. The railmotors consisted of a single coach with a small vertical boiler and proved to be a most capable unit.

Little has changed over the years as far as the station is concerned, although the goods yard is now a car park. The goods shed itself has survived, but is not in use. The number of vehicles in the car park gives an indication of Stroud's growing importance as a dormitory town, with commuter traffic to both Swindon and Gloucester. On 5 September 1991 Class '155' No 155311 departs with a Swindon-bound service. *Hugh Ballantyne/GD*

# Gloucestershire branches

DUDBRIDGE JUNCTION, NAILSWORTH BRANCH: The branch from Stonehouse, on the main Birmingham to Bristol main line, to Nailsworth was opened in 1867, passing to Midland Railway ownership by 1878. The line had several private sidings with freight services continuing until 1966, although the passenger service was to be one of the last economies of the LMS, being withdrawn 'temporarily' in 1947, never to be reinstated. A spur to Stroud was constructed in 1885, and the junction was at Dudbridge, where on 8 July 1955 ex-MR 0-6-0 Class '3F' No 43373 approaches the signal box *en route* to Nailsworth with a daily pick-up freight. The train had already visited Stroud, the line to which can be seen passing behind the signal box.

The railway layout is still clearly visible today; the cyclist is 'arriving' from Nailsworth whilst the 'Stroud line' diverges to the right. The location of the signal box can be identified by the two trees standing within 'the junction'. *Hugh Ballantyne/GD*

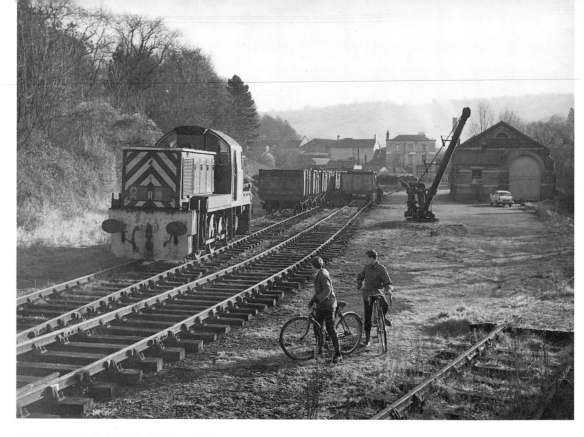

NAILSWORTH: Swindon-built Type 1 diesel-hydraulic locomotive No D9257 shunts the goods yard at Nailsworth on a sunny 3 January 1966; goods services to the town were to last only until 1 June 1966. In the background is the Railway Hotel, flanked on the right by the goods shed and crane. The passenger station, which closed in 1947, was situated on the embankment on the left, positioned thus because plans existed for the line to continue south. It was an attractive building, once used as the headquarters of the Stroud & Nailsworth Railway. At the Grouping there were six trains daily covering the 5¾ miles to Stonehouse. The locomotive was from a batch of 650 hp units which had a limited life on BR, due mainly to the work for which they were designed disappearing under the Beeching Plan. Following withdrawal, many found gainful employment with the coal and steel industries, and more recently some have found their way into preservation on the growing number of private railways.

The distinctive Railway Hotel remains and on the left the local fire brigade have erected their training tower. The goods shed has been demolished; the building on the right has, however, survived the closure, but was hidden behind the goods shed in the 1966 view. The trackbed of the branch is now utilised for recreational purposes. *Andrew Muckley/JW*

STROUD WALLGATE: The existence of Stroud Wallgate, and indeed the branch from Dudbridge Junction (see page 79), can be attributed to the problems of mixed gauges. Merchandise that was sent north suffered considerable delay and damage with the need for transhipment at Gloucester, where the change from broad to narrow (later called standard) gauge track took place, and this was a source of considerable annoyance to local merchants. Thus encouraged by the prospect of a lucrative source of freight, the Midland, which had already adopted the 'narrow' gauge, opened its own branch into Stroud in November 1885 for goods, and eight months later for passengers. The passenger service was never intensive and was suspended in 1947 as a post-war fuel economy.

However, the service never ran again and closure was confirmed in 1949. Freight traffic continued until 1966. The approach to Stroud Wallgate was by a curved viaduct, the end abutments of which are visible in this August 1964 photograph. At this time the old station was being used by British Road Services. Note that above the oil drum (centre left) one of the station nameboards appears to have survived.

The area around the station has changed considerably, the viaduct having been severed at the station end to make way for a new by-pass, which has also obliterated the station site. However, a large part of the viaduct remains with the arches in commercial use. Note the hill-top woodland to the right of the end abutment - this can be also be seen on the earlier view (far left). *Andrew Muckley/JW*

COALEY JUNCTION, DURSLEY BRANCH: The branch to Dursley opened in 1856, diverging from the Birmingham to Bristol main line at Coaley Junction. The station was situated within the junction, serving both branch and main line, as can be seen in this 8 July 1955 photograph. The guard of a main-line train looks out towards ex-MR 0-6-0T No 41720 and its short train, which will form the 4.30 pm to Dursley. Beyond the station on the Dursley side stood the goods shed.

The branch today consists of a short headshunt stopping well before the now rail-isolated goods shed, which none the less survives in good order. A stack of sleepers indicates where the signal box once stood. Passing on the main line is Class '37' No 37207 heading south with an engineers train. The loco carries the colours of the Civil Engineer, nicknamed the 'Dutch' livery as it resembles that of Netherlands Railways. *Hugh Ballantyne/GD*

DURSLEY: Although located near the town centre, the station at Dursley was neatly tucked between two factory buildings. The small but distinctive station building is on the left, the diminutive canopy being a feature. Note how the nearest chimney shows evidence of at least two additions in height to match the more ornate rear double chimney. A typical wrought iron lamp-post stands in the foreground and the platform bench seems in need of attention. Prior to the Grouping the branch had seven passenger trains each way daily, taking 9 minutes for the $2^{1}/_{2}$ miles to Coaley Junction. On 8 July 1955 ex-Midland 0-6-0T No 41720 awaits departure with the 4.10 pm service. The locomotive, together with sister engine No 41748, was a feature of the branch for some years, both retaining their open-backed cabs.

The site of the station is clearly evident today, although all trace of the buildings has gone. The left-hand gabled factory roof is the most distinctive feature common to both views, while on the right the traditionally styled factory has given way to a modern utilitarian unit. *Hugh Ballantyne/GD (courtesy of Petters Ltd)*

SHARPNESS BRANCH: The Sharpness Branch, which opened in 1875, was intended to form a through route via the Severn Railway Bridge to Lydney, also serving the nearby Sharpness Docks. The branch was 4 miles in length, leaving the Bristol main line at Berkeley Road. Rationalisation had taken place as long ago as 1931 when singling took place, which is evident from this 26 September 1964 scene, as Class '14XX' 0-4-2T No 1453 heads the 4.15 pm to Berkeley Road at Sharpness. The passenger service ceased later that year, some four years after the through route had been severed following the demise of the Severn Railway Bridge (see page 34).

Only the road overbridge at the north end survives to identify the station site, although the platforms can be identified beneath the thickening undergrowth. Ironically, the branch survives in part to serve the Nuclear Power Station at Berkeley, which is now in the early stages of de-commissioning. The closure of the branch can be predicted, although that day remains some years hence. *Hugh Ballantyne/GD*

TYTHERINGTON, THORNBURY BRANCH: In 1872 the Midland completed a 7¹/₂-mile branch from their main line at Yate (see page 89) to Thornbury, with intermediate stations at Iron Acton and Tytherington. It was not a busy passenger line with three trains per day each way in 1922, and it is of little surprise that the service was withdrawn in 1944. Complete closure came in 1966; some ten years earlier, on 15 April 1956, the 'REC Severn Venturer' railtour traversed the branch hauled by 0-6-0PT No 1625. The tour has paused at Tytherington for a 'photo-stop' and the station seems still in good repair despite having been closed for 12 years.

After closure the track was lifted, only to be reinstated in 1972 to serve the large ARC Quarry at Tytherington. Using rail recovered from the old Midland main line around Mangotsfield, and following the strengthening of bridges, the branch again saw traffic for the conveyance of limestone from the quarry. The present economic down-turn has caused the line to be mothballed, although there was a short burst of activity in the latter half of 1991, albeit only temporarily. the distinctive tree marks the location of the station and in the foreground is one of the new bridges installed to accommodate the heavier trains. Note the avenue of trees which has grown up on either side, effectively screening the railway from the expanding residential quarter of the village.
*Hugh Ballantyne/Robin Banks*

# Midland main line to Yate

STANDISH JUNCTION: Quadruple track typified the main line between Gloucester and Standish Junction; in fact, it was two sets of double track running in parallel. Metals to the west belonged to the Midland and to the east were Great Western. At Standish Junction three things happened: the two routes split, the Midland to Bristol and the Great Western to Swindon, and the junction allowed Great Western southbound trains to cross to the Midland and head for Bristol, and vice versa.

*Left* On 20 July 1963 an unidentified 'Hall' working a northbound express crosses from Midland to Great Western metals under the watchful gaze of the signalman in the typically Midland Standish Junction signal box. Note the LMS upper and GWR lower quadrant signals towards the rear of the train.

*Below left* With its train reporting number crudely daubed on its smokebox door, 'Jubilee' No 45602 *British Honduras* heads for Gloucester with the 9 am Paignton-Leeds on 9 August 1964. The signal box is behind the leading coach, and part of the train consists of Eastern Region stock. To the right of the locomotive is a shelter where the signalman apparently parks his motor-scooter.

*Above* Today the junction is situated on the Gloucester side of the road bridge, beyond which the route is now reduced to double track only. Passing the site of both signal box and crossovers are two Class '20' locomotives, Nos 20084 and 20170, heading an enthusiasts' special to Birmingham on 1 July 1990. *Hugh Ballantyne (2)/GD*

CHARFIELD, one of several intermediate stations between Gloucester and Bristol, is probably best remembered for a horrific crash which occurred on the night of 13 October 1928 when the Leeds to Bristol Mail ran through adverse signals and collided with a freight train. To compound matters, the Mail was then deflected into the path of another northbound goods. Gas, then used for carriage lighting, ignited and added to the carnage, with the resultant blaze raging for hours. Fifteen people perished, of which two were children travelling alone and who sadly were never to be identified. The station itself was served primarily by local services and was closed in 1965 when the trains were withdrawn. By 31 July of that year closure had already taken place as Brush Type 4 (now Class '47') No D1795 passes at the head of the 1.00 pm Paignton to Sheffield service.

The station buildings on the down side remain and the surrounding area is now used by a motor-car main agent. Buildings opposite on the up side have been demolished. However, following local residential growth and an identified need for commuting into Bristol, the station is to re-open in the near future with finance being provided by the local authority. For the moment, though, the encroaching trees along the embankment dictate a more head-on viewpoint as Class '47' No 47812 approaches with the 10.37 Paignton-Edinburgh train on 24 August 1991. *Michael Mensing/JW*

YATE: An unusual occurrence at Yate on 17 October 1965 as 0-6-0PT No 6435 leads 'Castle' 4-6-0 No 7029 *Clun Castle* and a Birmingham to Bristol Stephenson Locomotive Society special off wrong-line working. The pannier tank was on transfer to the Dart Valley Railway and private ownership. *Clun Castle* was also later destined for preservation at the Birmingham Railway Museum and an active main-line career. The original station at Yate had closed earlier that year, and the branch to Thornbury, which diverged to the left, closed in the following June.

By September 1991 Yate had been transformed: the station has re-opened as a 'park and ride' facility mainly aimed at Bristol commuters and plans exist for platform extensions to accommodate longer trains. The line to Thornbury had been reopened as far as Tytherington Quarry in 1972 (see page 85), although present low demand has caused the branch to be mothballed. On the main line Class '47' No 47802 approaches with the 08.40 Liverpool-Paignton. *Hugh Ballantyne/GD*

# Bath and the S&D

BATHAMPTON: Looking towards Bath from the east, the elegance of the Georgian terracing, for which the city is renowned, can be seen along the horizon, as Churchward designed 2-8-0 No 4707 approaches with a Westbury-bound freight on 15 September 1962. Consisting mainly of four-wheeled wagons, it contrasts sharply with the high-capacity vehicles typical of today. Note the bracket 'banner' repeaters which give advance warning of the goods loop situated prior to the junction with the Westbury line which at this point is less than 1 mile distant. The locomotive was introduced in 1919 and is one of only nine examples built.

Bath continues to dominate the horizon today but vegetation has grown considerably, necessitating a slightly different viewpoint, as can be judged by the position of the fence. The train is one of the few Regional Railways locomotive-hauled services, the summer 07.58 Cardiff to Weymouth, with Class '37' No 37254 in charge on 29 August 1992. The Civil Engineers livery on the Class '37' contrasts with the attractive Regional Railways colours on the coaching stock. *Hugh Ballantyne/GD*

SYDNEY GARDENS, BATH, a short walk from the centre of the city, were laid out in the 18th century as Bath was becoming a well-known and genteel spa. Designed to a high standard, the gardens were intended to match the best on offer elsewhere, particularly in London. Incredibly, especially in relation to today's attitudes, the railway was allowed to pass along the eastern boundary which resulted in the present attractive location from which to watch trains go by. On 4 August 1957 'Hall' 4-6-0 No 4947 *Nanhoran Hall* approaches Bath with a down express.

The gardens retain their timeless charm today, with perhaps the most notable change being the reduction of soot on the bridge and retaining wall. An IC125 service led by Class '43' No 43160 eases through the gardens in preparation for the Bath stop. These units entered squadron service on the Paddington to Bristol and South Wales services in 1976 and have been the most successful concept in rail travel in the UK for many years. *Peter Shoesmith/GD*

BATH SPA: It would appear that this is 'Castle' No 7006 *Lydford Castle* departing from Bath Spa with the down 'Bristolian' on 14 July 1962. In fact, the train is the summer Saturday equivalent, the 8.45 am to Weston-super-Mare, which ran to a slower schedule, but at the time was one of few regular steam-hauled services; for effect, Old Oak Common Depot added the pleasing touch of using the 'Bristolian' headboard. The normal rake of chocolate-and-cream-liveried stock has been strengthened by three maroon vehicles, the leading coach being an example of ex-GWR 1938 'Centenary' stock. Above the fourth coach is the distinctive elevated signal box, so positioned to afford a good view for the signalman over the long sweeping curve on which the station is situated. The sidings between the main running lines provided stabling for local trains laying over between turns. In the foreground is evidence of the recent extension of the up platform where the tarmacadam takes over from paving stones. Like many other Great Western stations, Bath had an overall roof when first built, but this was removed in 1897.

Today the basic structure remains; note also that the base of the old elevated signal box, which closed in January 1968, is still in situ. A floral display stands where the sidings were located as Class '43' No 43174 leads the 16.45 Paddington to Bristol Temple Meads IC125 service from the station along the elevated stretch of railway, which is a feature as it passes through the centre of Bath. *Hugh Ballantyne/GD*

OLDFIELD PARK was the first station west of Bath and catered for local traffic. Passing non-stop on 5 September 1970 is Class '52' No D1038 *Western Sovereign* in charge of the 13.40 Weston-super-Mare to Paddington express. First introduced in 1961, and nicknamed either 'Westerns', as all their names were so prefixed, or 'Thousands', after their numbering sequence of D1000 to D1073, they represented the ultimate design in the Western Region's diesel-hydraulic traction policy. The other Regions had decided on diesel-electric traction and thus the out-numbered hydraulics became non-standard and candidates for early withdrawal. The 'Westerns' were the last class to go, surviving until 1977 and enjoying an Indian Summer of popularity with the enthusiast and operator alike. Six examples have been preserved, although *Western Sovereign* was not so lucky, being an early casualty in 1973.

By August 1992 the general scene at Oldfield Park has changed little, but closer examination will reveal the removal of the up loop and subsequent encroachment of vegetation beyond the retaining wall. The down loop remains, nowadays for the use of trains of domestic waste from the nearby Avon Refuse Collection Yard. Class '43' No 43101 heading the 17.15 Bristol Temple Meads to Paddington express passes non-stop. *Hugh Ballantyne/GD*

TWERTON TUNNEL, BATH: Emerging from the castellated western portal of Twerton Tunnel on 14 July 1962 is BR 'Standard' 2-6-2T No 82037, heading the 1.12 pm Calne to Weston-super-Mare summer Saturday holiday train. Although very much a symbol of BR standardisation, the locomotive is on home territory, being a product of Swindon Works and part of a class of 45 engines introduced from 1952. Twerton itself is a suburb to the west of Bath, and lost its connection to the railway system in 1917 with the closure to its station. This was situated on an embankment on the Bath side of the tunnel, and after closure was used as an outlet for a number of commercial purposes.

Today the scene has changed little, with the loss of the signal box being the most notable feature. The train consists of china clay slurry tankers from Salisbury to Gloucester hauled by Railfreight Distribution Sector Class '47' No 47079, previously named *George Jackson Churchward* after the famous Great Western Railway Chief Mechanical Engineer. *Hugh Ballantyne/GD*

**BATH GREEN PARK:** The name of Bath Green Park station is firmly associated with the Somerset & Dorset Railway, although in fact it was originally the Midland Railway's terminus for its line from Mangotsfield. Having an impressive frontage, overall roof, two platforms and centre roads, it could on occasion be stretched by traffic demands. This was particularly so on summer Saturdays when holiday trains from the Midlands and the North would have to re-engine before heading south over the S&D. A more relaxed atmosphere is, however, evident on 11 September 1960 as S&D '7F' No 53804 stands at the head of an SLS Special bound for Templecombe. These fine locomotives were introduced in 1914 and were the most powerful on the line until the arrival of BR Standard '9Fs' in 1960. Eleven locomotives were built for the S&D and their Midland ancestry is plainly evident. The last member of the class was withdrawn in 1964 and two have found their way into preservation and main-line running.

Since its closure in 1966 the old station has been renovated to a high standard by J. Sainsbury and is used for exhibitions as well as car parking. (See also page 4) *Ellis James-Robertson/JW*

BATH JUNCTION (S&D): For the first half-mile from Green Park the S&D had to run over Midland metals before gaining its own line at Bath Junction. This view looks back towards Green Park; the station signal box is just visible behind the left-hand signal gantry post. Bath Junction signal box is situated behind the photographer, and the signalman there has given the S&D road to Class '9F' No 92001 heading the 7.45 am Bradford to Bournemouth West train on 14 July 1962. The locomotive was one of four '9Fs' drafted to Bath for the summer service and they were to prove most successful over the difficult gradients of the S&D, obviating the need to double-head the heavier trains. The tablet catcher is in position beside the cab steps, and the fireman can be seen awaiting the successful gathering of the single line tablet from the apparatus alongside Bath Junction box.

The trackbed is now partly used as a car park for the factory on the left and in the background the row of terraced properties remain distinctive by virtue of their pronounced chimneys. *Hugh Ballantyne/GD*

DEVONSHIRE TUNNEL: From Bath Junction the S&D line curved round to the south-east and climbed away at a ruling gradient of 1 in 50. This presented a stiff challenge to southbound trains, with the frequent need for banking locomotives to assist the heavier trains, particularly freights. Towards the top of this formidable climb was the additional obstacle of Devonshire Tunnel; its narrow bore and adverse gradient caused a most unpleasant environment for enginemen working southbound trains, particularly on the footplate of the inner locomotive when double-heading or when working the banking engine. The crew of ex-S&DJR Class '4F' 0-6-0 No 44558 should not suffer unduly, however, as their locomotive is working tender-first towards the tunnel mouth on 13 May 1964 with a short freight.

Today vegetation has closed in and the course of the railway is used as a walkway and cycle trail. The tunnel mouth is hidden behind the trees and bushes (centre). The severity of the gradient is still evident to visitors. *Michael Mensing/JW*

MIDFORD was the first station from Bath, some 4½ miles distant. On 1 February 1964 Station Master Cooper watches ex-S&DJR Class '4F' 0-6-0 No 44560 draw to a halt with the 3.20 pm from Bath to Templecombe local service. This was the last day for the station to be manned; it was to become an unstaffed halt until closure on 5 March 1966, the day on which the Somerset & Dorset Railway closed for ever. The signal box, from where this view was taken, remained until the end. Note the unusual S&D 'calling back' signal, which was used to allow up trains to set back off the single line on to the double-track section that commenced on the nearby viaduct. The locomotive is carrying the distinctive S&D lamp configuration for passenger trains, consisting of top bracket and left-hand buffer beam.

Today the platform remains in situ, the block wall corresponding to the similar structure in the 1964 view, although it appears to have been lengthened. The foreground, where Midford signal box once stood, is now the car park for the Hope and Anchor public house. *Hugh Ballantyne/JW*

**MIDFORD VIADUCT:** This is a classic S&D scene, showing the down 'Pines Express' entering the double-track section that commenced on Midford viaduct and continued to Templecombe. In the background is Midford station, whilst running beneath the S&D viaduct, also on a viaduct, is the Great Western's Camerton to Limpley Stoke line which closed in 1951, but is famous as the location for filming *The Titfield Thunderbolt* in 1952. The 'Pines Express' was the principal train on the route, running from Manchester to Bournemouth. On 15 August 1959 a combination of ex-LMS and Southern Railway power had charge of the train, with Class '4F' No 44424 leading unrebuilt 'West Country' 4-6-2 No 34102 *Lapford*. Southern 'West Country' 'Pacifics' were not allocated to the line, but were loaned to cover high seasonal demand.

By necessity, today's viewpoint is slightly different as the outlook from the road is now totally hidden by trees. The viaduct remains and the buildings right of centre are located above the site of Midford station and correspond to those above the viaduct in the 1959 photograph. *Hugh Ballantyne/JW*

# GW lines around Bristol Temple Meads

BRISTOL TEMPLE MEADS (1): Brunel's original terminus at Temple Meads opened in August 1840 with the completion of the main line to Bath. However, it was to be a further ten months before the through route to Paddington was inaugurated. The design of the magnificent train shed was a typical Brunel masterpiece, the 72-foot-span roof appears to be supported by hammerbeams which are, together with the colonnade, constructed entirely in timber; however, the roof is a cunningly disguised cantilever structure. Although medieval in appearance, the building was functional, containing offices, booking hall, boardroom and stabling facilities. It was later extended in 1865-78 by the architect Sir Matthew Digby Wyatt. Trains used the terminus for 125 years, in latter days predominantly Midland services. Closure came on 12 September 1965, since when most of the building has been used as a car park. This view, taken on 27 July 1965, shows the run-down building just prior to closure. The area beyond the wagons is the old engine shed above which the office accommodation often had the benefit of steam heating!

The building now enjoys Grade 1 listed status, being over 150 years old and still in virtually its original condition. BR has leased the building to the Brunel Engineering Centre Trust who have embarked on a painstaking restoration project which will turn the old station into a museum and exhibition hall. It was playing host to a model railway show in November 1990 when the 'present' photograph was taken. The old engine shed has been partitioned off, and a picture of Brunel now surveys the scene. *W. Potter/GD*

BRISTOL TEMPLE MEADS (2): Prior to 1878 Temple Meads consisted of Brunel's terminus and the Bristol & Exeter station which was positioned at right-angles to Brunel's train shed; a curve connected the two lines, and it was along this curve that a new through station was built in 1878. It was also a joint station, serving the Great Western, Midland and Bristol & Exeter Railways. The major feature of the new station was a superb 125-foot span overall roof which remains in situ today. At the eastern end the new roof joined with the new portal to the terminus station, as seen in this photograph taken on 12 June 1959. Standing in platform 9 is the last steam-hauled up 'Bristolian', with 'Castle' No 5085 *Evesham Abbey* in charge. The headboard contains the city crests of both Bristol and London.

The overall roof has recently been refurbished, but the view in general has been blighted by the Royal Mail's overhead conveyor system for transporting mail bags from the platforms to the sorting office next to the station on the south side; Temple Meads is a major inter-change point for mail trains. Note also that the nearest platform (now number 5) has been extended. Departing from what was once platform 9 is Class '47' No 47825 *Thomas Telford* with the 12.08 Plymouth-Manchester Inter-City service. *Hugh Ballantyne/JW*

BRISTOL TEMPLE MEADS (3): A further major rebuild took place between the wars, encouraged by Government subsidy to create jobs during the Depression. The result was a major expansion on the south side, beyond the original train shed and stretching into the nearby cattle market. Five new platforms were created as well as substantial infrastructure work in the vicinity. The enlarged station was not quite ready for the Great Western's centenary celebrations in 1935, but the occasion was marked by the inauguration of a new high-speed train between Bristol and London, the 'Bristolian', which departed from Temple Meads for the first time on 9 September 1935. More mundane traffic occupies the new platforms 1 and 2 in this 1950s view, in the shape of '45XX' 2-6-2Ts Nos 5540 (on the left) and 5546 (taking water on the right). The locomotives are operating local services, probably on the Radstock line.

The faded appearance of the old platforms reflect that they are no longer used for passenger services, and see only parcels traffic nowadays. A full renumbering of the platforms has taken place, reversing the old system so that now the low numbers are in the old station (north) and high numbers cover the more recent platforms of the 1935 extension. Modern signalling has enabled platforms to become bi-directional. On 14 October 1992 Class '43' power-car No 43148 is at the rear of the 15.15 IC125 service to Paddington. The Post Office sorting office is the modern building on the right. *Peter Shoesmith/GD*

BATH ROAD ENGINE SHED (82A) occupies the site of the old Bristol & Exeter depot built alongside that company's locomotive works. It was rebuilt in 1934 with a new ten-road shed, repair shop and coaling plant which was topped by a 135,000-gallon water tank. On 9 July 1960 a variety of ex-GW and BR Standard types can be seen outside the shed as 4 pm approaches. Bath Road closed to steam on 12 September of that year with the remaining locomotives being transferred to either St Philips Marsh or Barrow Road.

The depot was completely rebuilt at a cost of over £700,000 and reopened on 18 June 1962 as a diesel depot, since when most types of BR diesel traction have been serviced or repaired there. The old repair shop has been retained (left) whilst the new motive power depot stands on the site of the coaling plant. On the right part of the old steam shed has been retained next to which is the new office block. Parked around the depot are a selection of Class '47s' and '37s' in the liveries of Inter-City, the Civil Engineer and the Parcels Sector. *Hugh Ballantyne/JW*

**DR DAYS BRIDGE JUNCTION:** An unidentified 'Hall' winds around the curve at Dr Days Bridge Junction with a northbound train, taking the South Wales route from Bristol, which increased in importance with the opening of the Severn Tunnel in 1886. Merging from the left is the spur from North Somerset Junction on the Paddington main line, which allowed London trains direct access to the South Wales route without the need to reverse at Temple Meads. Thus it was possible to improve schedules to South Wales and avoid the long journey via Gloucester (it was to be a further 17 years before the direct line to South Wales via Badminton opened). To the right of the signal box are the extensive carriage sidings.

The junction has now been totally remodelled, with the line from Temple Meads now passing through the site of the carriage sidings. As an approximate guide, the bushes in the 'V' of the junction mark the site of the signal box. Class '47' No 47824 heads north with the 12.16 Paignton to Manchester service. *G. F. Heiron/JW*

LAWRENCE HILL: The Bristol & South Wales Union Railway of 1863 not only provided Bristol with a suburban train service but eventually, with the opening of the Severn Tunnel, a further main-line connection. (Originally the line ran to New Passage on the Severn where a steamer connection was made to South Wales.) Lawrence Hill was the first station from Temple Meads, 1 mile distant, the buildings being just visible above the first coach of the express hauled by 'Grange' 4-6-0 No 6810 *Blakemere Grange*. To the right is an extensive goods yard and shed, whilst off the picture to the right, on an embankment, is the Midland main line. *Blakemere Grange*'s crew would be working hard to get a good run at Filton Bank.

In 1984 the route from Dr Days Bridge Junction to Filton Junction reverted to double track. The goods yard has closed and is now used as a car park, but a cement terminal has been established which is rail connected. Heading north through the station is Class '43' No 43071. *David Wall/JW*

FILTON JUNCTION: Having negotiated Filton Bank, the driver of 'Castle' No 7019 *Fowey Castle* will be easing his locomotive for the long curve into Stoke Gifford. The train is the up 'Bristolian' on 19 May 1959. Filton Junction was a substantial station with the tracks on the far side leading to Patchway and the Severn Tunnel. A spur was also provided to the Avonmouth line.

Not quite, but nearly! The platform from which the 1959 photograph was taken has now been removed and the line to Stoke Gifford can be glimpsed on the extreme left. The view today is taken from the end of the island platform looking towards the Patchway line as Class '158' No 158815 pauses with the 12.01 Bath-Swansea train, one of only seven to serve the station on weekdays. The basic platform shelters give a good indication of its decline, although the wrought iron fences are a reminder of better days. *Hugh Ballantyne/GD*

# The Midland in Bristol

BARROW ROAD ENGINE SHED: This late 1950s scene conveys well the atmosphere of a large steam shed. Barrow Road was the Midland Shed in Bristol, located to the east of Temple Meads and a few yards along the same road that spans Dr Days Bridge Junction. Its allocation was smaller than the two Great Western depots, and in January 1954 had charge of 55 locomotives. This is the view looking over the parapet of Barrow Road bridge, which conveniently overlooked the shed and the Midland main line (extreme left). A mixture of ex-Midland and LMS types can be seen, along with a couple of ex-GW pannier tanks. One engine of note, parked between the left-hand chimney and the lamp-post, is 'Jubilee' No 45690 *Leander* which after withdrawal was rescued from the scrapyard and completely restored to main-line condition. An active main-line career followed, and the locomotive is now at the Severn Valley Railway awaiting overhaul.

Barrow Road Shed closed in November 1965 and was demolished the following year. This is the scene today from Barrow Road bridge today with the whole vista having changed. Off the picture to the right is the remains of the old line to St Philips Station (closed 1953) which survives today for trains to reach the household refuse collection terminal located on the branch. *G. F. Heiron/GD*

KINGSWOOD JUNCTION: The Midland exit from Bristol was equally as difficult as the Great Western's line via Filton, with a stiff climb to Fishponds. Midway was Kingswood Junction where, on the right, ran the line from Ashley Hill Junction (on the Clifton Down-Avonmouth branch). In May 1964 'Castle' Class 4-6-0 5091 *Cleeve Abbey* battles against the gradient with an express for the Midlands. The locomotive carries the reporting number 1M37: the figure 1 indicates that it is a class 1 train (an express), the M that its destination is on the London Midland Region and the 37 is the train identification number. Diesels had the benefit of a neat four-character blind system, but the fast diminishing stock of steam locomotives often had their number chalked on the smokebox door - on No 5091 the code 1V51 has not been cleaned off from a previous working, the V indicated a working destined for the Western Region.

It is difficult to imagine that a railway ever ran through the location today. The old main line is a cycleway, partially hidden by the hedge, and a new housing estate has been built on the land that was occupied by the junction, with the course of the Ashley Hill line off to the right behind the white stuccoed house. The only clue to the past is the row of terraced houses in the left background. *David Wall/JW*

**FISHPONDS:** The first Midland station from Temple Meads was Fishponds, some 3 miles distant. It was mainly served by local stopping trains and was built in traditional Midland style; on the left is a goods yard of sufficient size to justify its own signal box. Drifting through the station is ex-MR 4-4-0 No 40501 on a short freight. This design of loco dated back to 1912 and, in various forms, was common all over the Midland system.

The site of the goods yard has now been totally cleared, and the road overbridge in the distance is all that indicates the location of the station, of which the platforms remain. The actual railway formation is a much-used cycleway. *E. T. Gill/GD*

MANGOTSFIELD: At the Bristol end of Mangotsfield station, the Gloucester and Bath lines converged at West Junction. This view dates back to the late 1950s and shows 'Jubilee' 4-6-0 No 45573 *Newfoundland* heading the southbound 'Devonian'. In the background is Carsons Chocolate Factory, a well-known landmark, behind which ran a chord between the Gloucester and Bath routes to create a triangle of lines. The station had four platforms, with the main building situated within the junction, and was of classic Midland design.

The station closed in 1966, and has been partially demolished, with the platforms and some walls of the building remaining. A cycleway now follows the Bath route and in the background is the outline of the chocolate factory, although nowadays it is used for other purposes. *G. F. Heiron/JW*

MANGOTSFIELD NORTH JUNCTION: Rounding the curve from the station at Mangotsfield North Junction is 'Jubilee' 4-6-0 No 45577 *Bengal* heading a northbound express for Birmingham. The train consists of coaching stock painted in the then standard 'blood and custard' livery. Coming in from the left is the chord from the Bath line, and the rear of Carsons Chocolate Factory can be seen above the first coach. Mangotsfield North Junction signal box is on the left.

It is still possible to walk the old trackbed from Mangotsfield station site to North Junction, and the chord to Bath is also accessible. All trace of railway infrastructure has, however, gone, but the outline of the chocolate factory remains a feature. *G. F. Heiron/JW*

WESTERLEIGH (1): The Midland Railway's main goods yard was situated at Westerleigh on the north-east outskirts of Bristol, near Yate. The sidings were laid on the east (down) side and consisted of 24 roads split between two yards. They were closed in February 1965, the traffic being transferred to the nearby Stoke Gifford Yard. Although on different routes, a spur from the Midland at Yate to the Great Western Badminton line just north of Westerleigh gave equally easy access to Stoke Gifford. On a warm August day in 1964 a relief to the northbound 'Cornishman' passes Westerleigh hauled by 'Castle' 4-6-0 No 4082 *Windsor Castle*. The photographer's vantage point is the steps of the signal box.

Traffic was reintroduced to Westerleigh in 1985 when Avon County Council opened a rail-served household refuse disposal point. Later, in 1991, a new Murco oil distribution terminal opened, bringing regular oil block trains from West Wales. On 10 August 1992 Class '60' No 60025 *Kinder Low* draws the 17.45 return empties to Robeston out of the Murco terminal. Also on site is a BR Civil Engineers depot. *David Wall/Don Gatehouse*

WESTERLEIGH (2): At the north end of the yard the line enters a shallow cutting on the approach to Westerleigh village. This view was taken on a sunny day in May 1964, but not a good washing day for the occupants of the terraced houses due to the volcanic exploits of BR Standard Class '4' 2-6-0 No 76038 as it lifts a long raft of wagons from the yard.

The line is now singled as traffic is reduced to the daily household refuse train, a thrice weekly oil train plus traffic to the Civil Engineer's depot. Note how the end terraced properties have been combined and extensively renovated. *David Wall/JW*

NEAR WARMLEY: The line from Mangotsfield to Bath Green Park was upgraded because of its growing importance as a cross-country route via Bath and the Somerset & Dorset. The Midland was thus able to establish a valuable traffic flow from the North and Midlands to the South Coast. The line also served communities on the northeast side of Bristol, and this scene is just to the south of Warmley with BR 'Standard' 2-6-2T No 82001 leading a Bath Green Park-Bristol via Mangotsfield train in August 1964. Bath to Bristol via the Midland was 3 miles longer than the Great Western alternative, and it was to be the latter which ultimately survived.

The Midland line lost its passenger service in 1966 and closed to freight in 1971. The vegetation has now closed in, but the trackbed is still in good use as a cycleway. On the right a new housing estate has been built and the school remains visible in the background. To the south of this spot, at Bitton, a preservation scheme exists. Known as the Avon Valley Railway, it offers a steam service at weekends and is well worth a visit. *David Wall/JW*

# The Badminton Route

CHIPPING SODBURY: BR Standard Class '5' 4-6-0 No 73027 is admired by father and son as it pauses at Chipping Sodbury with the 11.23 am Swindon to Bristol Temple Meads stopping service on 25 March 1961. Beyond the footbridge on the up side is a busy goods yard with a substantial goods shed. The yard was closed in 1966, some time after the passenger station had closed following the withdrawal of the local service.

The platform on the up side remains, as does the typical Great Western station building; the latter, like the goods yard, is used by the Civil Engineers department, although the centre of the yard is a caravan store. Both fast lines remain in use but the down platform loop has been removed, although the up loop has been retained for access to the goods yard. Class '43' No 43027 leads the 12.00 Paddington to Swansea IC125 service on 11 September 1991. *Hugh Ballantyne/GD*

COALPIT HEATH was one of two stations between Westerleigh and Stoke Gifford on the Badminton route. Typically for the Great Western it was a quite substantial station serving a small community and was an early closure in 1961. However, a few years earlier everything seems in good order as 'Castle' No 7023 *Penrice Castle*

hurries by heading the 8.00 am Pembroke Dock-Paddington express. Coalpit Heath had been reached by Bristol's first railway, a horse-drawn tramway from the River Avon at Avonwharf in 1835, built to transport coal from local mines.

The station building survives on the down side, and note how the old canopy has been retained as part of a post-closure wooden extension. The platforms also survive, with the gap beneath the far platform locating the site of the signal box. High Speed Trains are usual on this stretch of line, working to London and the North via Birmingham. On 14 October 1992 Class '43' No 43014 heads the 09.25 Penzance to Edinburgh through the station. Note that the power-car has buffers, one of the few so fitted as part of push-pull working trials with electric locomotives. *G. F. Heiron/GD*

STOKE GIFFORD YARD opened with the advent of the Badminton route in 1903. Situated at the eastern edge of Filton Junction, it had ideal access to Bristol, Avonmouth, South Wales, the Midlands and London, and was enlarged in 1914 to provide 14 up roads and 10 down roads. The yard is not, however, at full capacity in this May 1964 photograph, which shows BR Standard Class '9F' No 92118 departing eastbound with a rake of mineral wagons. In the background is a BR Class '08' shunter and an ex-GW '47XX' Class 2-8-0.

The yard closed in October 1971 and much of the land on the up side was used for the car park to serve the new Bristol Parkway Station, which can be seen in the background. Opened in 1972, it soon became very successful and has been a model for similar stations around the country. A measure of its popularity can be gained by the sheer size of the car park, although Saturdays are quieter, as this view taken on 12 October 1992 indicates, with Class '43' No 43157 passing at the head of the 12.20 Bristol-York service. The station is also a major interchange point, serving both the Paddington-South Wales main line and the important South West-North via Birmingham cross-country route. The sidings that remain in the old down yard now belong to the Civil Engineer's Dept. *David Wall/JW*

# Lines to Avonmouth

STAPLETON ROAD (NARROWAYS HILL) JUNCTION: A Class '63XX' Type 2 diesel-hydraulic locomotive leads a lengthy mixed freight on to the Avonmouth line at Stapleton Road in May 1964. The class were introduced from 1959 onwards and were intended for intermediate passenger and freight duties. Their career span was, however, short, the first withdrawal being in 1967, and the class was extinct by January 1972. The final member, No 6357,

had been in service for only six years and one month when it was withdrawn on 12 December 1968. After leaving the South Wales main line, the Avonmouth branch climbs to Ashley Hill Junction and heads west via Clifton Down Tunnel before joining an earlier line from Hotwells (beneath Clifton Suspension Bridge) at Sneyd Park Junction. The spur to Hotwells closed in July 1922 to make way for the Portway, a major road development to the docks.

In the present-day view a two-car DMU with motor brake No 53948 leading heads on to the now singled branch at what is known today as Narroways Hill Junction. The branch was singled as part of the Bristol resignalling scheme which was completed by 1972.
*David Wall/GD*

SEA MILLS: After emerging from Clifton Down Tunnel, the line enters the western end of the Avon Gorge before reaching Sea Mills, situated on the bank of the River Avon at a point where it is joined by a minor tributary. The background houses indicate that this is a prosperous area of Bristol. The train is an afternoon service from Bristol Temple Meads to Avonmouth on 16 June 1958 hauled by an ex-GW 'Mogul' 2-6-0 No 5311, and consisting of suburban stock.

Singling took place in 1972 with the introduction of the Bristol resignalling scheme, which also involved the removal of the down platform. Today all trains use the remaining platform which has contrasting styles of waiting shelter. In September 1991 a two-car DMU consisting of Nos 54097 and 53602 arrives with a Bristol Temple Meads to Severn Beach service. The main station building (off the picture to the left) still survives. *E. T. Gill/GD*

AVONMOUTH DOCK: In order to serve Avonmouth Dock a loop was created off the main line which by-passed Avonmouth station and allowed direct access to the considerable sidings and the docks' internal railway. At Gloucester Road Crossing the loop was very close to Avonmouth station, where both railways ran parallel, the two lines crossing Gloucester Road just a few yards apart. On 9 June 1964 diesel-hydraulic Type 2 No D6356 eases a mixed freight over the level crossing. Note the large dockside warehouse and concrete silo in the background and the wartime air raid shelter next to the signal box.

All traces of the railway have now been removed, the lower viewpoint being dictated by the crossing footbridge having been dismantled. The warehouse, silo and air raid shelter, however, remain. The docks are still active - indeed, they are set to see a large increase of traffic when the new coal import terminal is completed.
*E. T. Gill/JW*

CROSS HANDS HALT: The extension of the railway to Pilning via Severn Beach opened to goods in February 1900, but the passenger service did not commence until 1922. The line crossed the Severn Tunnel close to its eastern portal, and utilised part of the old route to New Passage Pier. On 9 May 1958 BR Standard Class '3' 2-6-2T No 82001 approaches Cross Hands Halt with the 5.20 pm Bristol Temple Meads-Severn Beach train, which will have travelled via Patchway and the main line before taking the low level line at Pilning. Note also that the train consists mainly of LMS stock, which is a reminder of the Midland Railway's influence in this predominantly GW area.

The distinctive church pin-points the scene today, and the course of the railway is still clearly evident. *Michael Mensing/JW*

PILNING (LOW LEVEL): Pilning had two stations only a few yards apart, one serving the South Wales main line whilst Low Level accommodated the Severn Beach and Avonmouth trains. The branch left the main line at the eastern end of the stations, with the branch falling away slightly before crossing the Pilning Road and entering Low Level station. This was a rudi-mentary affair consisting of one wooden platform and a couple of buildings, the nearest being a tim-ber-built waiting shelter. Whilst most northbound trains terminated at Severn Beach, seven services continued through to Pilning just prior to the withdrawal of the train service in November 1964; freight continued until 1968. On 28 June 1960 BR Standard 2-6-2T No 82044 draws to a halt with the 5.50 pm Bristol Temple Meads to Severn Beach and Avonmouth train.

The station area has now been developed, but note that the cross-ing gates remain (in the back-ground, right of centre) in the posi-tion to which they were returned after the passage of the last train. Pilning main-line station remains open, just, with a service of one train each way per day. *E. T. Gill/GD (courtesy of Mr Stocker)*

HENBURY: The opening of the Badminton route created the need for a more direct access to Avonmouth, which resulted in the Filton line being opened in 1910. The branch was one component of a three-way junction, whereby the main line from Badminton gave access to Temple Meads to the south, and to South Wales via the Severn Tunnel to the west, and vice versa. Thus trains from both London and the Midlands could reach Avonmouth without the need to pass through Bristol. Henbury was one of four passenger stations on the line and presents a neat and tidy appearance in this late 1950s view as 0-6-0PT No 3748 pauses with an Avonmouth train. Judging by the number of passengers leaving the station, the train was well used.

After losing its passenger service in 1964, the line reverted to freight-only operation and was singled as part of the Bristol resignalling scheme. Recently, Avonmouth has been identified as the western gateway for imported coal, with Didcot Power Station being a prime destination. To cater for the projected dozen-plus trains per day, the branch is again being doubled. At Henbury, part of the old platform has been cut away in preparation for the extra track as Class '60' No 60024 *Elizabeth Fry* passes with a train of liquid petroleum gas from Furzebrook to Hallen Marsh on 30 June 1992. *E. T. Gill/GD*

HALLEN MARSH JUNCTION: The line from Filton via Henbury joins the Severn Beach route at Hallen Marsh, which as can be seen from this July 1986 view is situated in the heart of the Esso petroleum plant at Avonmouth. At that time the area was controlled by manual signal boxes and lower quadrant semaphore signals. Hallen Marsh signal box was of typical Great Western design and is in contrast to the hi-tech plant on the horizon. The train is the 17.25 ICI Severnside to Dringhouses (York) freight consisting of empty vans for Rowntrees Chocolates in York, and the distinctive 'Cobra' potash wagons returning empty to Boulby on the North East coast above Whitby. Hauled by Class '37' No 37125, the train is winding off the Severn Beach line prior to running round and heading north via Filton.

Only six years separate these two views, but by 1992 the semaphores have gone, Hallen Marsh signal box has been demolished and the track rationalised. The train is the same as that seen at Henbury on the previous page. The Class '60' is BR's freight locomotive for the future, introduced to compete with the American designed and built and designed Class '59s' which are heavy-haul locomotives privately owned by Foster Yeoman and ARC. *GD/GD*

# Bristol Harbour lines

BRISTOL HARBOUR LINES (1): The Canon's Marsh goods branch opened in 1906 and served the north side of Bristol's Floating Harbour, which had been cut from the Avon to allow vessels to navigate nearly to the city centre. The branch ran from Ashton Junction, on the Portishead line, over a swing bridge at the entrance to the Floating Harbour, then along the northern perimeter of the harbour to Canon's Marsh itself. Ashton Swing Bridge had two levels - the upper carried the roadway and the lower the railway. It was last opened in 1936 and became a fixed structure in 1953. The sidings at Canon's Marsh ran close to the cathedral, which can be seen on the far left of this February 1959 scene as 0-6-0PT No 3776 heads towards Ashton Swing Bridge with a goods train. The branch at this point is sandwiched between the harbour and main road. Note the dry dock on the far side of the harbour, which was destined to become the home of an illustrious vessel.

The branch closed in June 1965, with the course of the railway at this point now a pleasant promenade with good views of the harbour and its star resident, Brunel's SS *Great Britain*, which is now being restored after a dramatic rescue from the Falkland Islands. The ship is open to the public, and one of many attractions in the area. *E. T. Gill/GD*

BRISTOL HARBOUR LINES (2): Cumberland Basin is at the western end of the Floating Harbour and close to Ashton Swing Bridge. The railway curves sharply at this point, negotiating a level crossing before reaching the swing bridge. On 20 November 1963 '63XX' Type 2 diesel-hydraulic locomotive No D6351 stands at the signal cabin awaiting the road over the level crossing before proceeding to Ashton Junction. The Floating Harbour forms the backdrop with the twin towers of the cathedral just visible above the rear cab of the locomotive.

The 1963 photograph was taken from a now demolished footbridge, so today's view is from a vantage point further back. It does, however, permit the location of the level crossing to be included (foreground) as the railway ran between the two nearest houses. Note the building with the gable at the end of the waste ground, which is the same structure as that in the 1963 view, to the right of D6351. Considerable re-development has taken place around the harbour, with the masts of the *Great Britain* and the cathedral visible in the background. *E. T. Gill/JW*

# Portishead branch

CLIFTON BRIDGE: The Portishead branch, which opened in April 1867, was 11$^1$/$_2$ miles in length from Bristol Temple Meads. It left the Exeter main line at Bedminster Junction and wound its way through the Avon Gorge, passing beneath Brunel's Clifton Suspension Bridge. Clifton Bridge Station was located at the entrance to the gorge, which can clearly be seen in the background spanned by the impressive bridge. On 16 March 1961 BR Standard 2-6-2T No 82035 awaits to depart with a Temple Meads-bound service. The station had an impressive building, with platform canopies of an attractive 'half barrel' design. The River Avon runs to the right of the station whilst in the background is the Hotwells district of Bristol, which was the destination of the original line from Avonmouth.

The viewpoint remains the same but what today's photograph does not reveal is the absence of steps on the footbridge causing the photographer to balance precariously on the metal lugs which once supported the step planking! The location is now tightly hemmed in by trees although one platform is visible plus some of the track. The station house has gone but still dominating the background is Brunel's famous bridge. *E. T. Gill/GD*

PILL: Beyond the gorge and some 7¹/₂ miles from Temple Meads is Pill, an area now expanding due to the proximity of the nearby M5 motorway. Back in February 1962 modernisation is also apparent as a DMU consisting of units Nos 55032 and 56292 working the 1.15 pm to Bristol crosses with the 1.00 pm Bristol-Portishead service hauled by 0-6-0PT No 7729. Passenger services survived until September 1964, and as recently as 1985 the branch was used for a steam shuttle service as part of the GW150 celebrations.

The cutting is now very overgrown, and the right-hand platform has disappeared beneath trees and bushes. The left-hand platform has fared a little better with the edging slabs still visible. Note that the track is still in situ: essentially the branch is mothballed, as plans for a Metro tramway or light railway system have been discussed. Some years ago a scheme was considered to link the branch to Royal Portbury Dock, but this came to nought. *Hugh Ballantyne/JW*

PORTBURY was the penultimate station on the branch, although it was remote from the settlement it served. The station house is an impressive two-storey building with a small goods yard which ran behind the building at the Bristol end. On 13 November 1958 the branch-line train approaches hauled by 0-6-0PT No 9626. Note the signal box and semaphores in the left background. Portishead itself was 2¹/₂ miles distant; its original railway station was taken over by the enlarged power station during the Second World War, and a new station opened in 1954, the first new peacetime station to be completed. Today even this has been totally obliterated beneath a petrol filling station.

The station house at Portbury is now in private hands and has seen a number of improvements. A lawn covers the site of the goods yard, but the overgrown track and platform are still evident, although the M5 motorway now separates the station from Portbury itself. *E. T. Gill/JW*

BRISLINGTON: The Bristol & North Somerset Railway from Bristol to Radstock and Frome opened in 1873, and was absorbed into the Great Western in 1884. Stations served local communities along the essentially rural route, although the movement of coal from the North Somerset coalfield was another important source of traffic. Brislington was the first station from Bristol, and was situated some 2¹/₄ miles from Temple Meads. The facilities provided were basic, consisting of one platform and station building to cater for a low-density service. Opposite is the goods yard which is a hive of activity, catering for general merchandise as well as domestic coal. On 24 October 1959, ex-GW 2-6-2T No 5536 departs for Bristol with the 10.50 am service from Frome.

Remarkably the station remains largely intact today. The platform edge can clearly be identified whilst the station building appears in relatively good order, only the canopy having been removed. Note also the telegraph poles which have also survived. *Hugh Ballantyne/JW*

WHITCHURCH (AVON): A classic rural station scene at Whitchurch, which opened as recently as January 1925 and served the nearby village. Its GWR heritage is typified by the 'pagoda' waiting room situated on the single-platform halt. However, the traction by 31 October 1959 was of definite BR origin, with Standard Class '3' 2-6-2T No 82040 drifting to a halt with the 10.50 am Frome to Bristol Temple Meads service.

Although the foreground has been cleared, obliterating any sign of the railway, the background hill and left-hand tree identify the location today. The bridge, visible behind the train in the 1959 view, remains, although now totally hidden by vegetation. It is also likely that the distinctive foreground tree (right) and that partially hidden by the pagoda shelter are the same. *Hugh Ballantyne/JW*

PENSFORD VIADUCT: The major feature of the line was a 16-arch stone viaduct bridging the valley at Pensford. The village is located on the far side of the viaduct, as indicated by the church tower just to the right of the locomotive buffer beam. Pensford station can be seen at the far end as an ex-GW 2-6-2T No 5508 heads south with the 2.53 pm Bristol Temple Meads to Frome service on 14 March 1955. The viaduct was built to accommodate double track, and although the line catered for the extensive North Somerset coalfield, doubling never proved necessary. Following the demise of the passenger service in 1959, freight remained until July 1968, closure then being hastened by a serious landslip near Pensford.

The viaduct continues to dominate the scene today, remaining in good order. At the far end, the site of the station and goods yard show evidence of redevelopment. *Hugh Ballantyne/GD*

RADSTOCK: The passenger service survived until 2 November 1959, and nine days earlier 0-6-0PT No 5771 stands in Radstock (GW) with the 2.53 pm Bristol to Frome service. The GWR station was in the centre of the town; at that time Radstock still had two stations, as the Somerset & Dorset station was only a short distance away. Radstock was also a centre within the North Somerset coalfield, where the last colliery to close in 1973 was at Writhlington, situated close to the town.

The right-hand platform survives, and by necessity our viewpoint today is from there, as the left-hand platform is now situated somewhere in the middle of dense undergrowth. Note that the distinctive shop, which was situated next to the level crossing, remains. *Hugh Ballantyne/JW*

# Bristol to Weston-super-Mare

NAILSEA & BLACKWELL is located 7$^1$/$_2$ miles south of Bristol on the Exeter main line, and dates back to the opening of the Bristol & Exeter Railway in 1841; the stone building is of original B&E construction. Approaching on 5 May 1959 is 'Hall' Class 4-6-0 No 5926 *Grotrian Hall* heading the up 'Merchant Venturer', which ran from Weston-super-Mare to Paddington via Bristol. The station is sited on an embankment, and recent attention to the up platform is evident. A varied bunch of passengers await their train, including what appears to be a permanent way gang (at the signal box end), judging by their shovels. The lady nearest the camera appears to be signalling to the train, but alas the photographer did not report the outcome!

The only surviving building today is the shelter on the down side, although the windows have been filled in. All the original buildings on the up side have been removed, leaving the traveller to compare the respective delights of old and new-style waiting accommodation. As with Yatton (opposite), the station caters for a growing demand from Bristol commuters and has recently been provided with a new car park. On 17 September 1992 the 13.54 Bristol to Taunton train approaches formed by a Class '101' 'Heritage' DMU set. *E. T. Gill/JW*

YATTON (1): In a view taken from the station footbridge looking south, we see 'Hall' Class 4-6-0 No 6940 *Didlington Hall* arriving with the 11.28 am Bristol service on 4 June 1960. On the right is the main station building, which is again of original B&E design. The 'half barrel' platform canopies are slightly unusual, and note that the station still boasts a platform newspaper kiosk. The signal box is of non-standard Great Western design, with the ornate barge-boards being a feature. It was also a particularly busy box, with the main line, two branches and goods yard to regulate.

The up side of the station remains virtually unaltered today, but the original down platform canopy has been removed. However, the station is maintained in good condition and caters for increasing commuter traffic for Bristol. On 17 September 1992 Class '158' No 158822 hurries past with the 12.00 Paignton to Cardiff service. *E. T. Gill/JW*

YATTON (2): Yatton's importance can best be judged by noting the station nameboard, which proclaims 'Junction for Cheddar Line and Clevedon'. The Cheddar line, with roughly seven services daily, was the least active, as the Clevedon branch peaked at roughly 30 daily return journeys. Behind the nameboard can be seen 0-4-2T No 1412 standing in the Clevedon bay platform; the Cheddar platform is on the extreme right, with the goods yard adjacent. Passing through on the main line is Class '28XX' 2-8-0 No 2875 heading a southbound fast fitted freight. Note the exceptionally long bracket on the platform-sited signal gantry, necessary due to the protruding canopy.

Today the Clevedon bay remains, but the Cheddar line platform and goods yard now serve as a car park. The station nameboard still refers to 'Yatton for Clevedon', although the only connection now is by road. On 17 September 1992 Class '158' No 158829 eases away from the Yatton stop with the 12.55 Cardiff to Taunton train. The '158s' are the most modern units in service with Regional Railways, and were introduced to work semi-fast 'Express' services, particularly on cross-country routes. *E. T. Gill/JW*

139

CLEVEDON (1): Clevedon is situated on the Somerset coast and is within 15 miles of Bristol. In July 1847 a 3½-mile branch to Yatton was opened to connect with the main line and thus provide an excellent link to the developing city of Bristol. However, the lack of a good beach meant that Clevedon could not rival Weston-super-Mare, but none the less it prospered as a dormitory town. In latter years there was an intensive shuttle service to Yatton, amounting to as many as 30 return trains daily operating from before 7.00 am to after 11.00 pm. The Great Western station was situated close to the town centre and comprised a single platform with awning, booking hall and water tower. On 4 June 1960 ex-

GW 0-4-2T No 1463 arrives from Yatton. The signal box stands at the end of the platform and controls access to the adjacent goods yard. Note the impressive and substantial goods shed of GWR design, while the wagons probably conveyed domestic coal. On the platform just beyond the end of the awning is an attractive goose-necked gas-lamp, so typical of the time.

The branch closed on 3 October 1966, and today the station site is occupied by a supermarket, this Sunday afternoon view of the car park is not representative of normal activity! One feature that remains to connect the two photographs is the terraced housing on the right; in the 1960 scene part of the roof and the upper windows of the same block can be glimpsed beyond the right-hand wagons. *E. T. Gill/JW*

CLEVEDON (2): This view taken on the same day shows No 1463 standing in the platform with the two-coach auto-train from Yatton. The auto-train method enabled the locomotive to push as well as pull, being driven from a cab in the rear coach when pushing, thus avoiding the need to provide run-round loops and minimising operating costs.

An inspection of the houses on the background hill will confirm the location, as the right-hand building now hides the row of shops to the right of the station nameboard in the 1960 photograph. *E. T. Gill/JW*

CLEVEDON (WC&PR): Clevedon was the headquarters of the Weston, Clevedon & Portishead Railway, which was better known affectionately, and probably a little irreverently, by its initials, 'the WC and P'. Opened to Weston in December 1897 and Portishead in September 1907, the line had a chequered history resulting mainly from financial difficulties. Indeed, for most of its existence it was operated in receivership under the stewardship of the legendary Col H. F. Stephens, who specialised in running independent railways. The WC&P ran for some 14 1/4 miles, with 12 stations plus several 'request' stops. *Bradshaw* of 1922 indicates four daily return journeys plus a further five intermediate services. This classic location involved street-running through a part of Clevedon, aptly known as Station Road. In July 1935 Manning Wardle-built 0-6-0ST No 3 *Weston* passes W. H. Smith's Circulating Library with a four-wheel passenger vehicle in tow. Note the steps to enable passengers to alight at roadside halts.

The modern Clevedon seems to have changed little, with the buildings in Station Road showing no significant alteration. It is good to see that W. H. Smith retains its prominent corner position. *The late S. W. Baker, collection of C. G. Maggs/JW*

WESTON-SUPER-MARE: The railway was a major factor in the growth of Weston-super-Mare as both a seaside resort and dormitory town for Bristol. Initially, though, the people of Weston were not too keen on the railway and allowed the main line from Bristol to Exeter to pass them by, being content with a mere branch to serve their needs, opened in 1841. Demand, however, led to the branch being doubled by 1866, together with the provision of additional excursion platforms. The layout changed drastically in 1884 when the branch was converted into a loop with the provision of a new through station, called 'General', while the existing Locking Road became the excursion station. This classic scene dates back to the late 1950s as 'King' Class 4-6-0 No 6018 *King Henry VI* eases a rake of chocolate-and-cream coaches from General station, heading for Bristol and Paddington. Note the activity in Locking Road, partly obscured by the exhaust.

Rationalisation commenced in 1964 when the Locking Road excursion platforms closed, followed by singling of the loop in 1972 as part of the Bristol area resignalling scheme. A much simplified layout exists today with, ironically, Locking Road now a coach and bus park. The branch has seen recent investment, with General station being refurbished and new stations opened at Weston Milton and Worle to cater for commuter demand. In April 1990 Class '155' No 155313 departs from Weston with a train to Bristol. Note the unchanged skyline. *G. F. Heiron/JW*

# INDEX OF LOCATIONS